GREATNESS IN THE COMMONPLACE

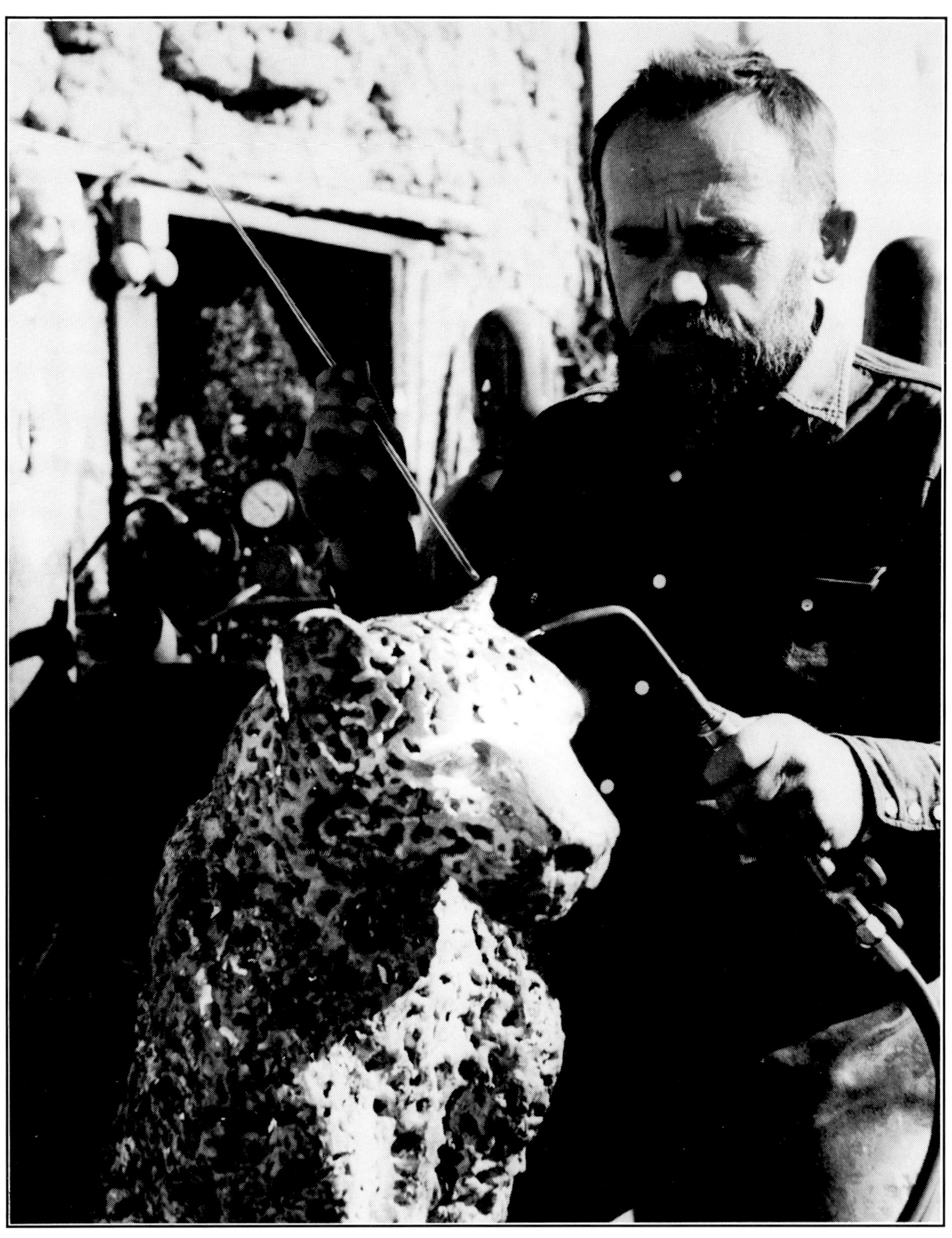

BORIS GILBERTSON

GREATNESS IN THE COMMONPLACE

The Art of

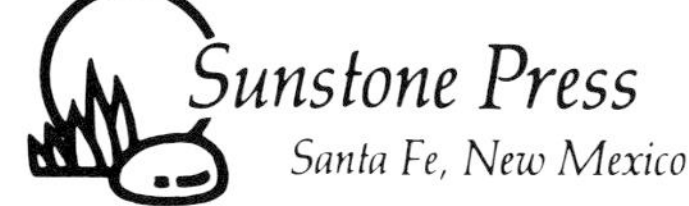

by

Charlotte White

Sunstone Press
Santa Fe, New Mexico

First Edition

Printed in the United States of America

Library of Congress Cataloging in Publication Data:

White, Charlotte, 1914-
Greatness in the commonplace.

1. Gilbertson, Boris, 1907-1982. 2. Sculpture,
American. 3. Sculpture, Modern--20th century--
United States. I. Title.
NB237.G53W45   1987   730'.92'4   87-7132
ISBN: 0-86534-115-X

Published in 1988 by SUNSTONE PRESS
Post Office Box 2321
Santa Fe, NM 87504-2321 / USA

COVER: ELIJAH, (Detail) bronze/corten steel (1971), 16'

ACKNOWLEDGEMENT

Phyllis Seidkin and Steve Kestrel provided
invaluable encouragement and help
in the production of this book.

CONTENTS

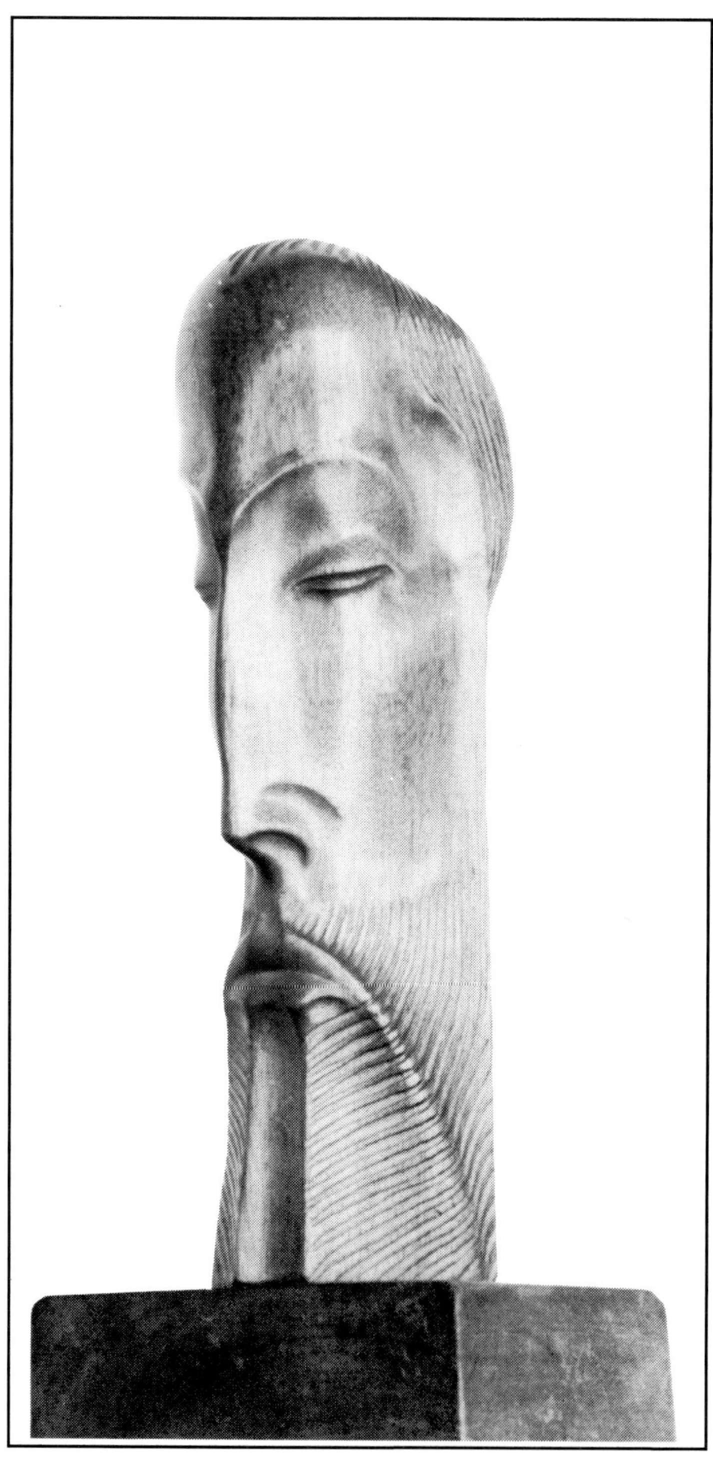

PHILOSOPHER, Honduras mahogany (1933) 12'' x 3''

FOREWORD

Boris Gilbertson had no liking for record keeping. So any retrospective such as this depends largely on the attentiveness of those who kept records for—or of—him. He was a private person; his work was his life.

Of his early years, he disclosed little, either in newspaper interviews or in the interview he granted to the Archives of American Art in Detroit, Michigan, in 1964. To a large extent, he turned away serious questions with humor.

Only after his death in 1982, when a few old clippings saved for him by his mother were found in his studio-workshop, was it possible to document some of his early achievements for contemporary audiences.

What is known from these interviews is that Gilbertson was born in Evanston, Illinois, in 1907, into a Norwegian-Russian family—his father's family Black Norwegians, his mother's Russian Cossacks. His father was a chemical engineer whose work took him throughout the Midwest. As a result, the family traveled constantly during Gilbertson's childhood. However, during those growing-up years, he also spent much time with his grandparents and other relatives near Chicago. That everyone whittled and carved, or drew, or quilted, or built furniture, often using animal motifs from Russian folklore, made a strong impression on him.

Adventurous, and loving travel, Gilbertson left home when he was barely fifteen, riding a "rattler" from Chicago to Denver. There he got a job with the Union Pacific Railroad, and worked also for the Denver and Rio Grande, sometimes with explosives in tunnel opening. It was while using his railroad pass that he first saw Santa Fe, New Mexico.

"With money in my shoe," Gilbertson would return to Evanston each fall where, after graduation from high school, he enrolled in the University of Chicago to study physics. A chance stroll around the corner from the university to the Oriental Institute, however, resulted in realization that art, not physics, was his future. Several men were unloading a large crate, and when Gilbertson saw emerging from it a massive Persian bull's head—from the excavations at Persepolis—his decision was made. Enrolling at the Art Institute of Chicago, he began his true life's work.

In 1960 he settled in Santa Fe, New Mexico where he lived and worked for the last twenty-two years of his life.

Gilbertson epitomized his Russian and Norwegian ancestry. Strong, rebellious, independent, and—though he would never admit it—

a romantic, he was above all an artist. He had a great sense of humor. He was sensitive, compassionate, touched and inspired by all things brought his way. To him, life was a wonderful adventure: he could have lived forever and never lacked interests and ideas. ''Boredom'' was not in his vocabulary.

He could do anything with his hands, from working on the most delicate jewelry to repairing a car, from building a workshop to creating evocative Chinese ink drawings, from executing small art pieces to carving huge stone sculptures or working corten steel into massive objects. He had equal dexterity in all mediums—stone, wood, slate, and metal.

Gilbertson believed that art should be anonymous: ''A work of art should be able to stand on its own, unlabeled by its creator. I will let my work speak for itself. The message is a simple one, whose hope is to reveal something great in the commonplace.''

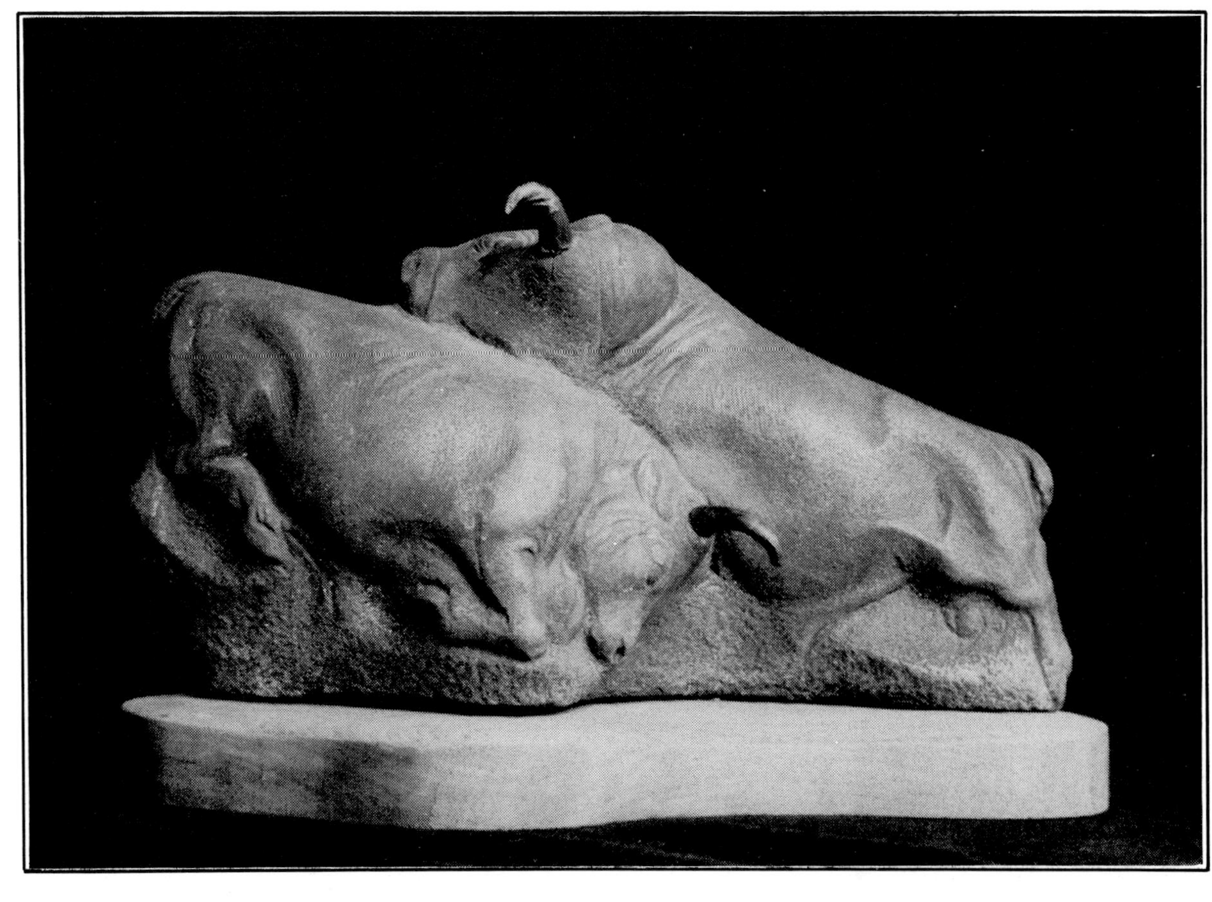

FIGHTING BULLS, limestone   (1953) 7'' x 13''

STONE

Most of Gilbertson's early work was stone, either Indiana limestone, marble, or Carthage marble, which is oolitic limestone. For small pieces, he used hand tools; for his large commissions, he used a compressor and air tools.

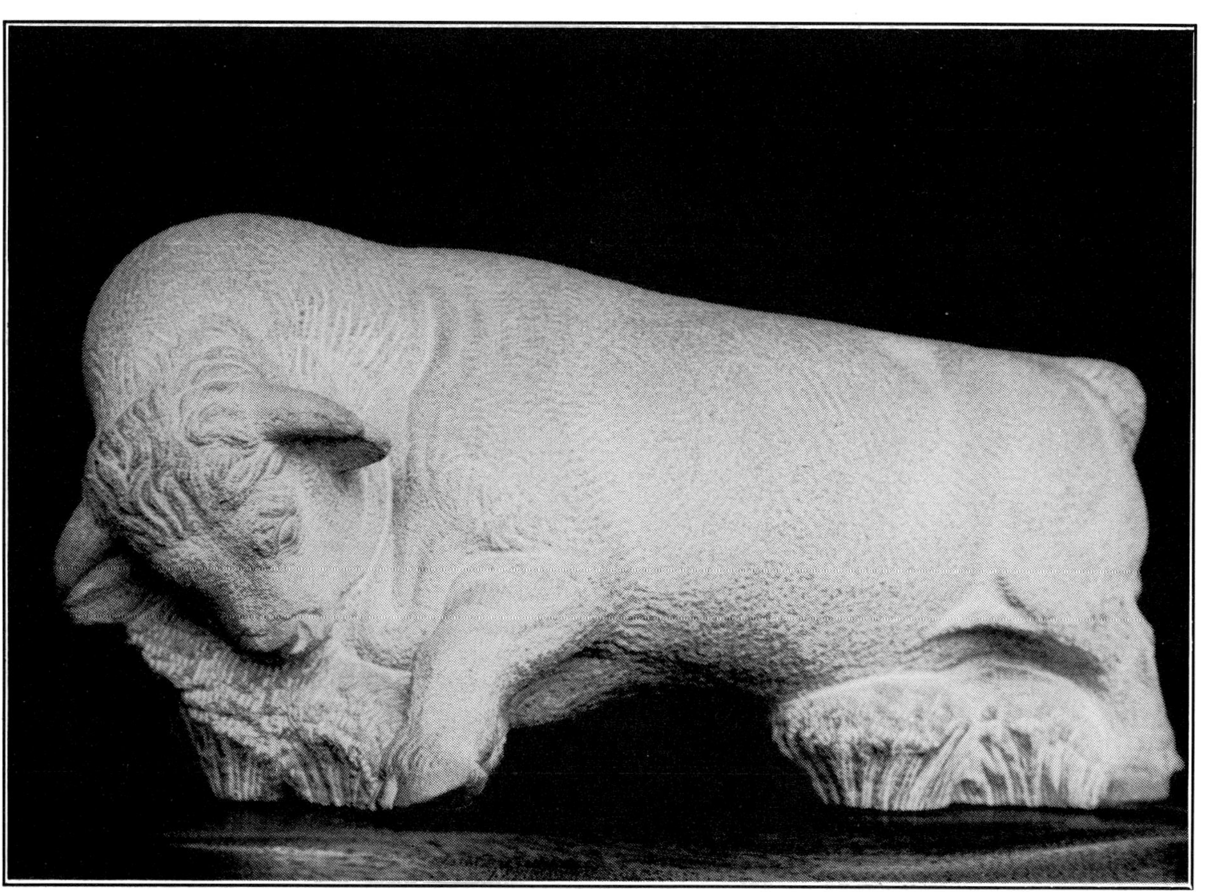

BULL, limestone (1936) 9'' x 19''

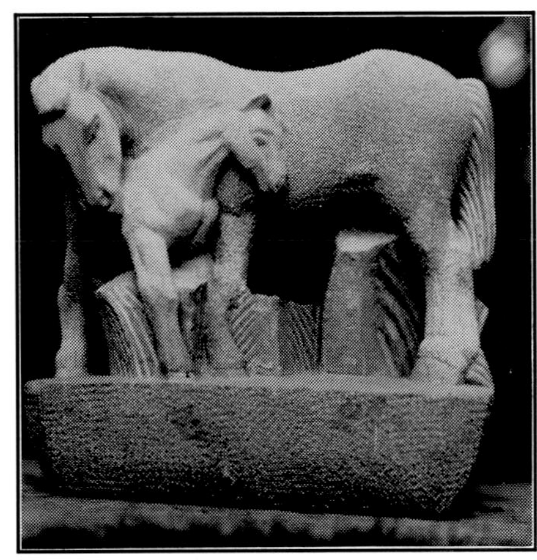

MARE AND COLT, limestone
(1938) 12'' x 19''

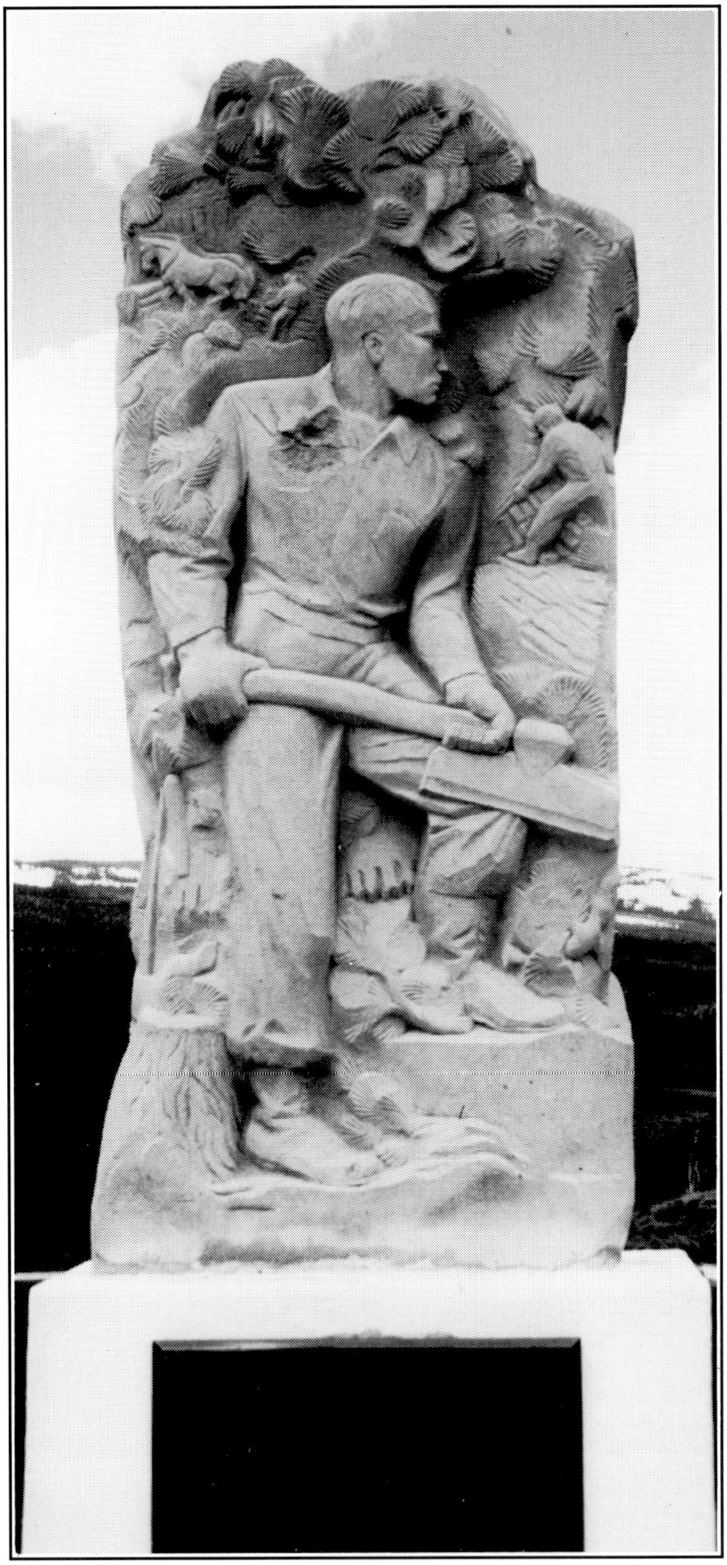

MEMORIAL TO WOODS AND RIVER MEN,
limestone (1946) 9' x 3'

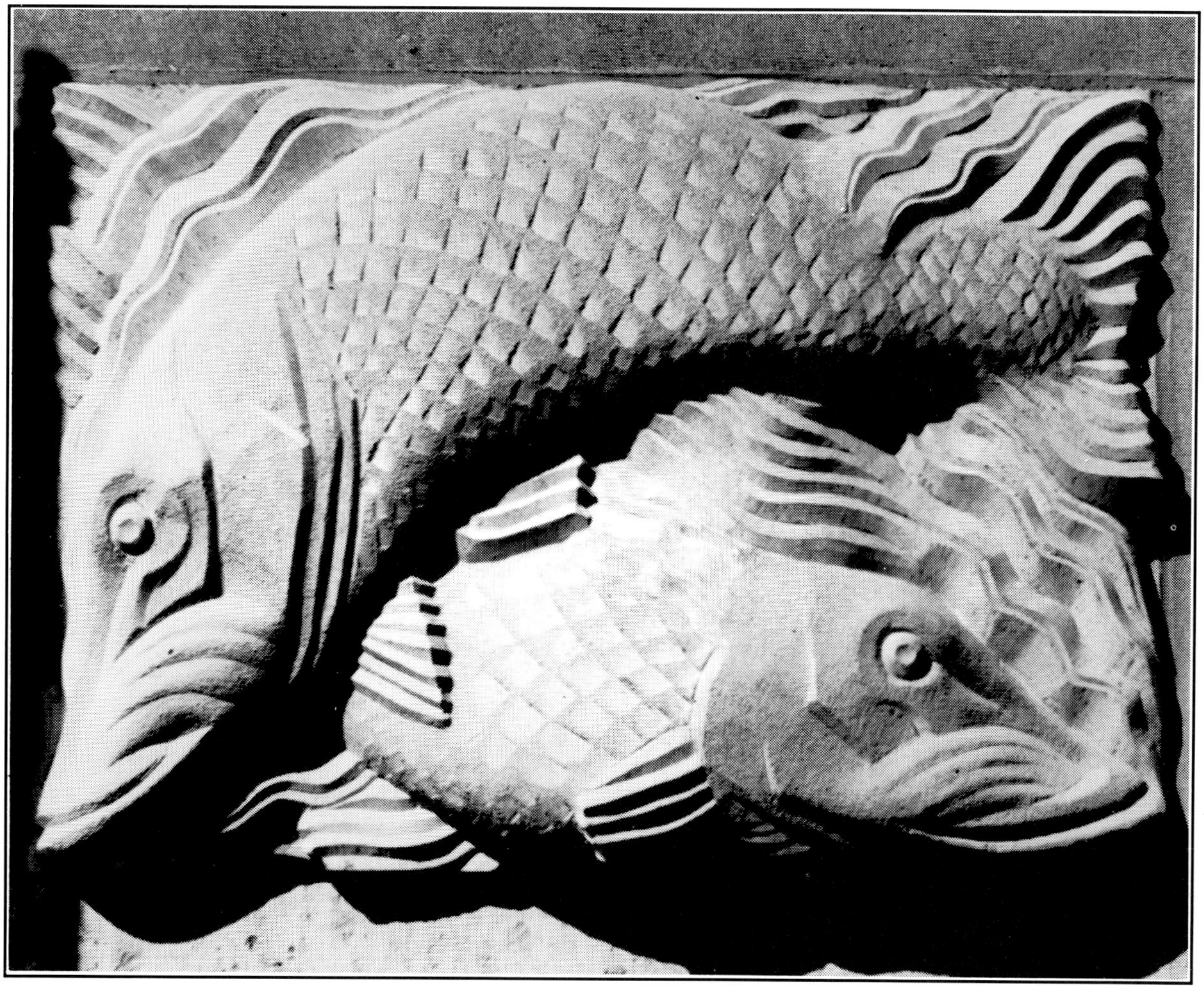

FISH, limestone (1938) 30'' x 42''

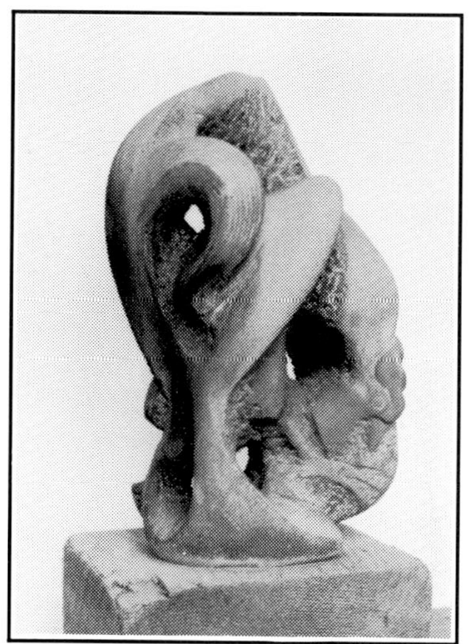

FIGHTING COCKS, limestone (1954) 15'' x 8''

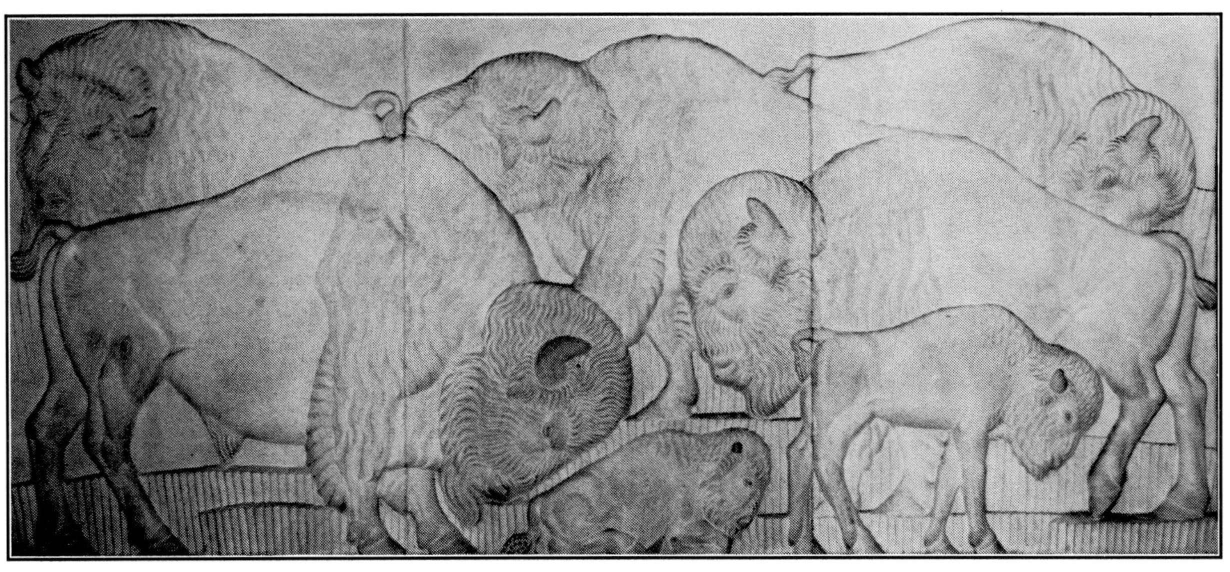

BISON RELIEF, Carthage marble (1939) 5′ x 13′, Photo Habs, Hugo Brooks

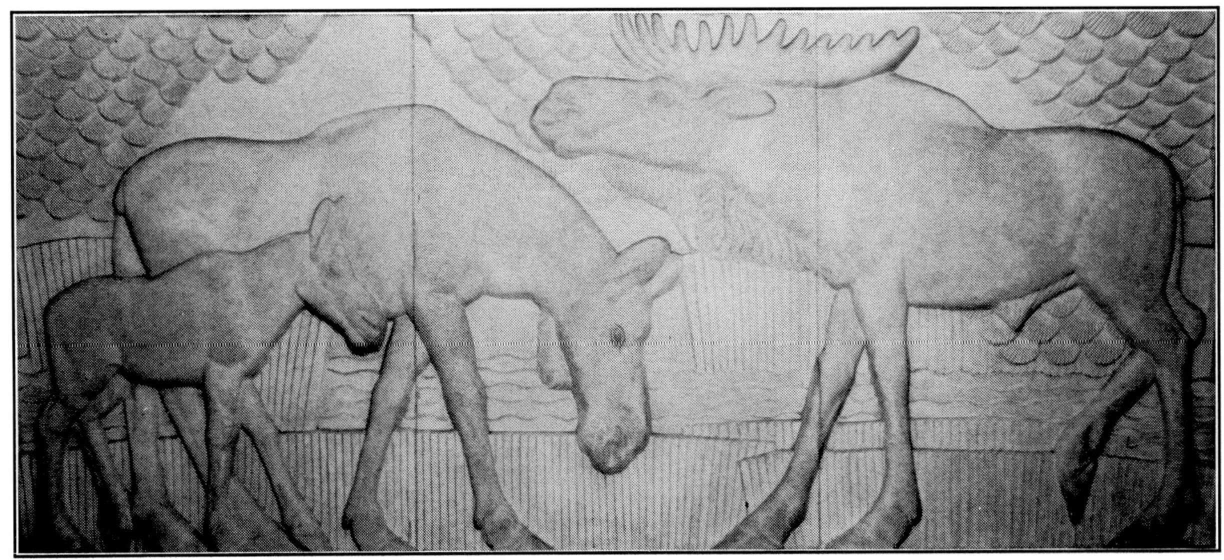

MOOSE RELIEF, Carthage marble (1939) 5′ x 13′, Photo Habs, Hugo Brooks

SLATE

The smaller slate carvings were executed with razor-sharp hand tools, the larger ones at least roughed out with air tools. For the larger pieces, Gilbertson used old blackboards, heavy and thick, salvaged from demolished schools. His study of calligraphy is evident in these pieces.

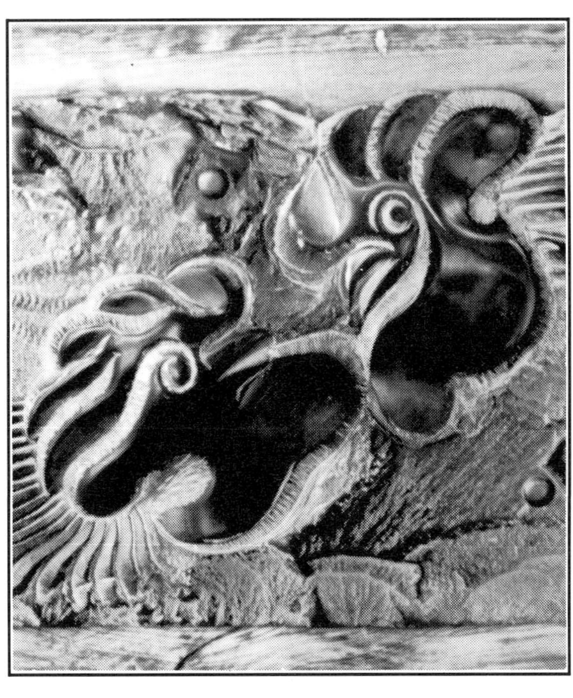

FIGHTING COCKS,
detail, slate (1956)

FIGHTING COCKS, slate (1956) 9½'' x 72''

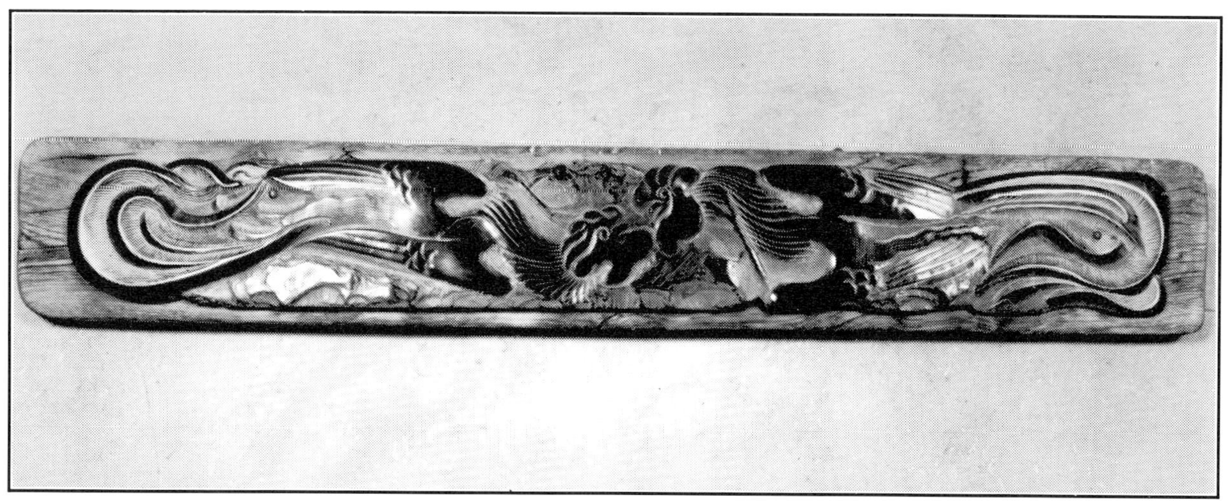

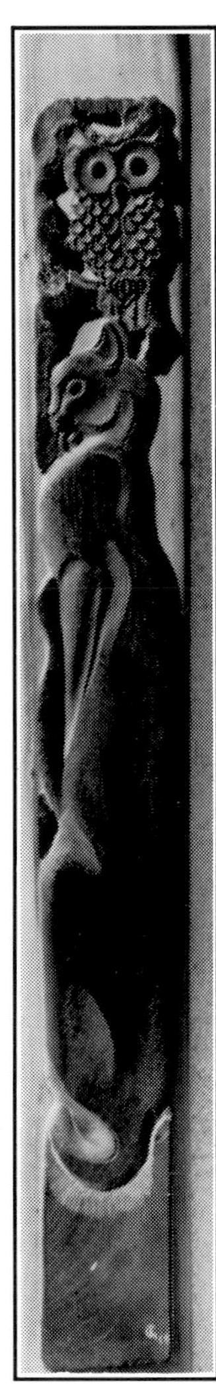

OWL AND PUSSYCAT,
slate (1955) 24″ x 12″

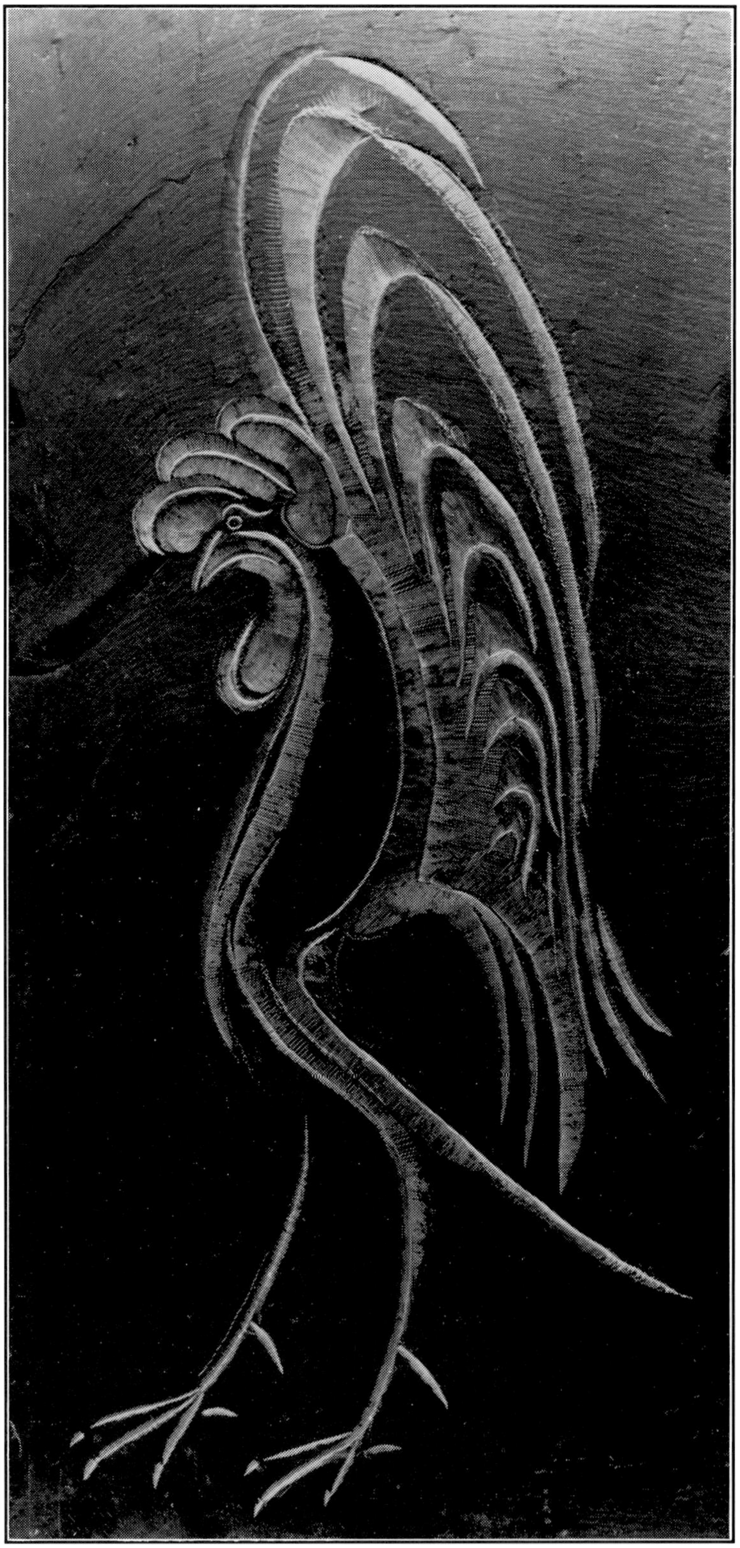

ROOSTER, slate (1960) 24″ x 10″

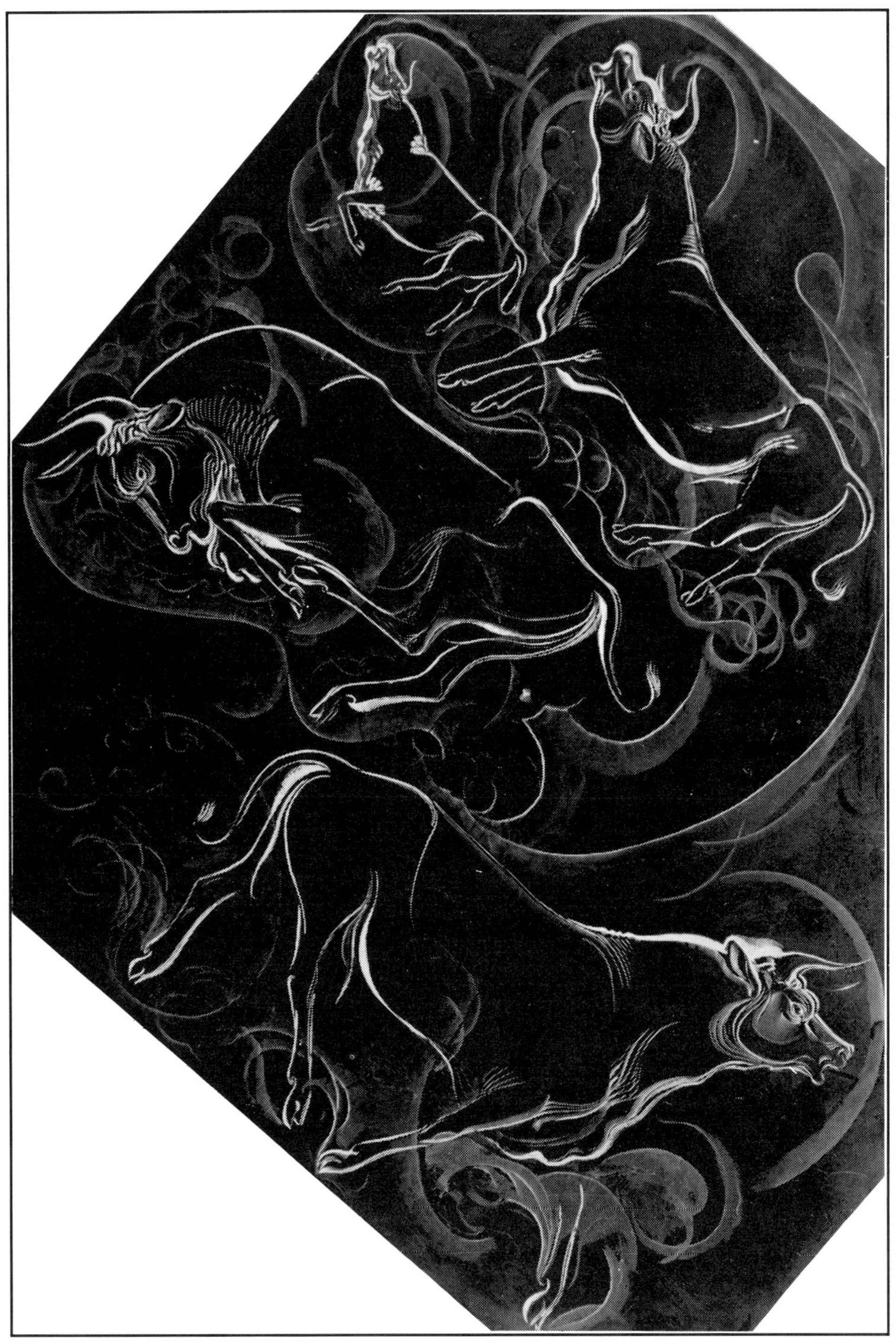

FIGHTING BULLS, slate with gold leaf (1951) 36'' x 36''

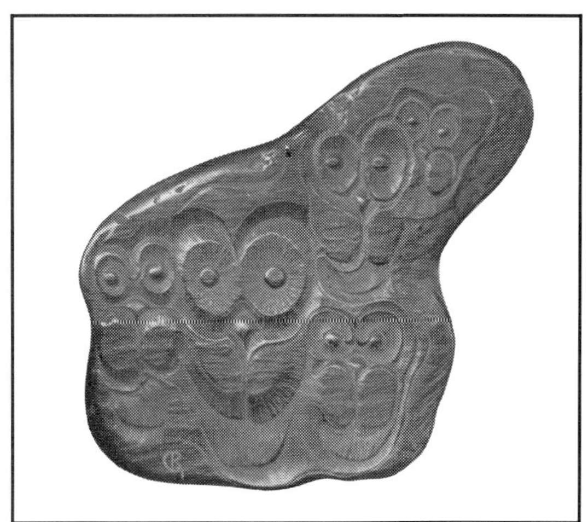

FIVE OF A KIND, slate (1978) 18'' x 12''

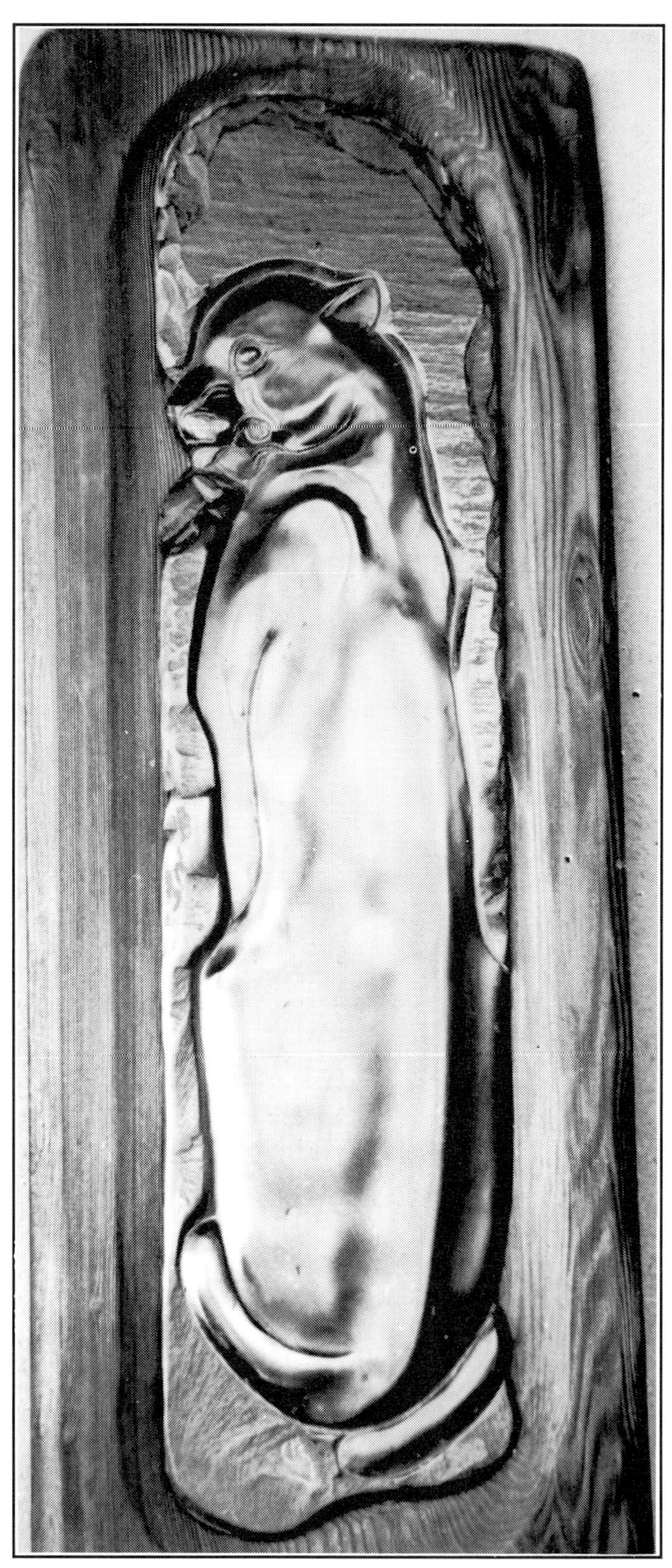

PUMA, slate (1956), 30'' x 11''

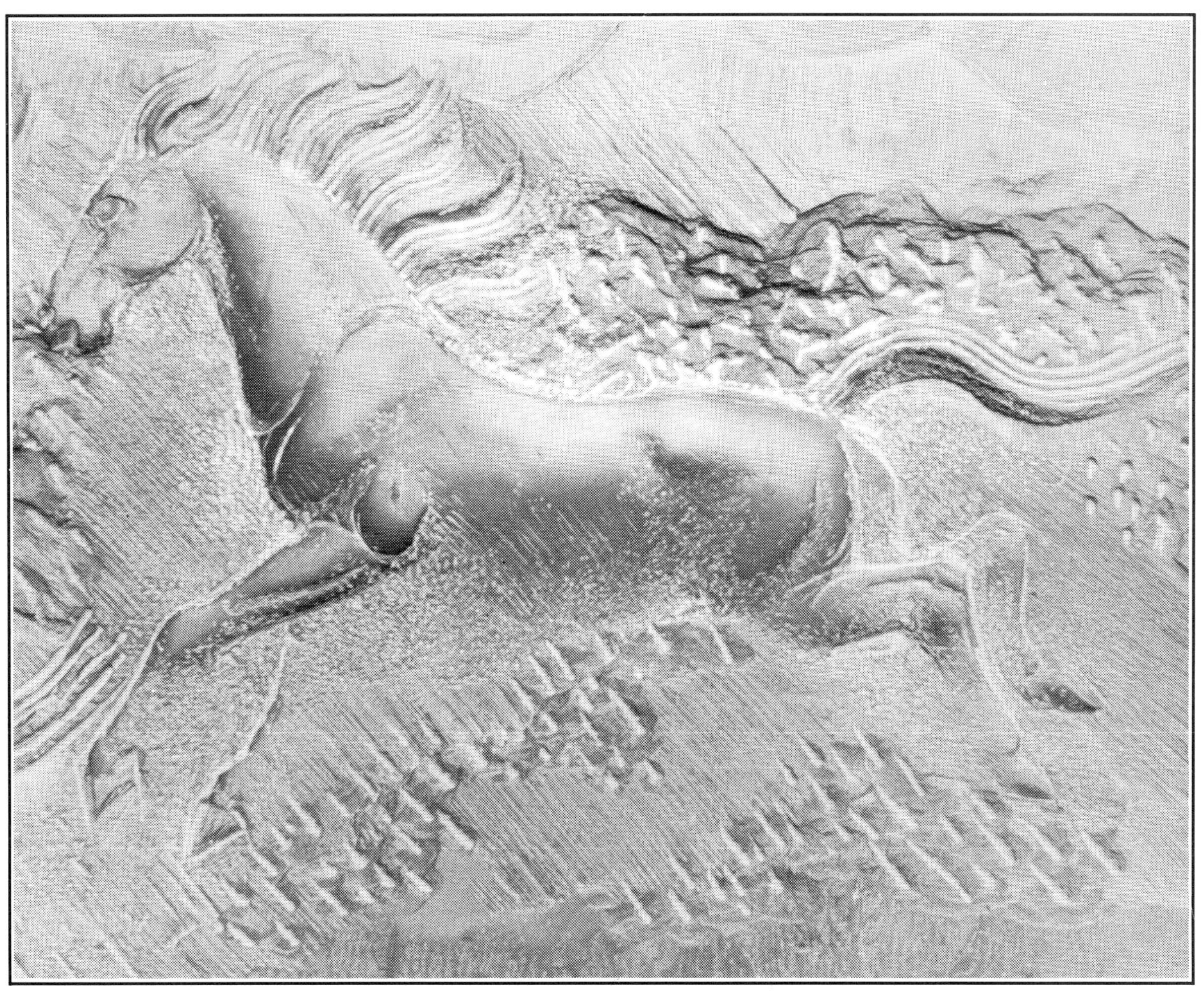

HORSE, detail from panel, slate (1965) 9'' x 48''

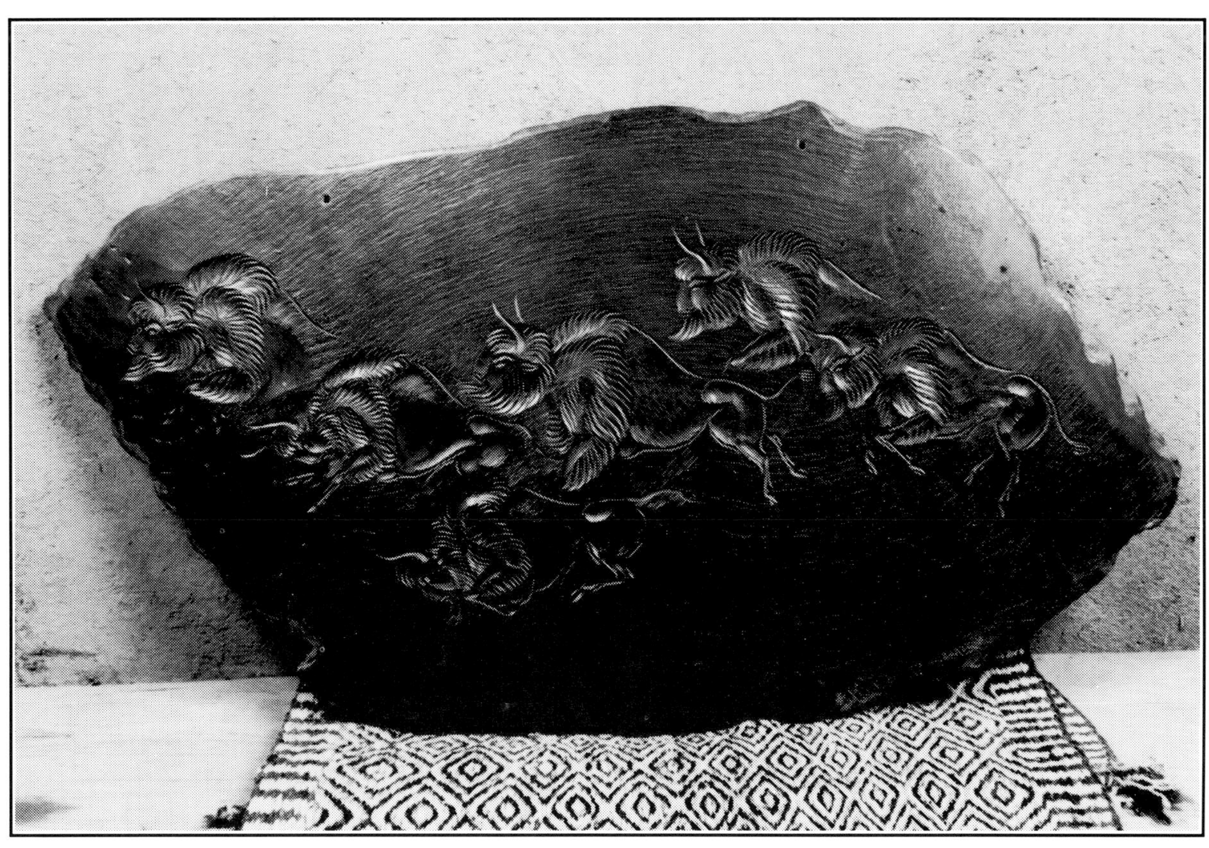

BISON, slate intaglio (1955) 25'' x 45''

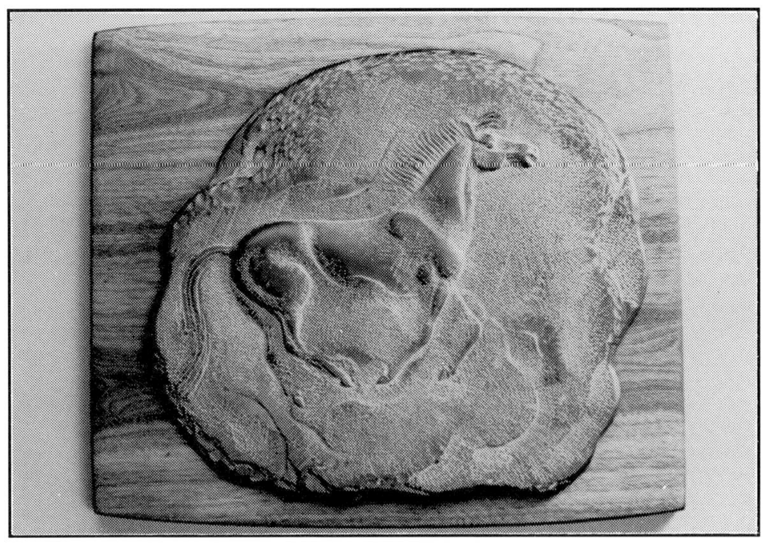

HORSE, slate (1970) 10'' x 12''

CHESS

Probably from childhood, Gilbertson had been a chess player. His feeling for the game shows in these works. The thirty-five-foot panel and two standing figures were commissioned by the architect Maurice Webster for the outdoor Chess Pavilion on Lake Michigan in Lincoln Park, Chicago. The cast bronze chess pieces (king and four rooks) were to have been part of a chess set of silver and gold commissioned by Dr. John Fleming. Casting was dictated by the number of similar pieces; this was the only work in which Gilbertson planned to use this technique. Failing health prevented him from completing the set. The several pieces that he finished in wax were cast after his death.

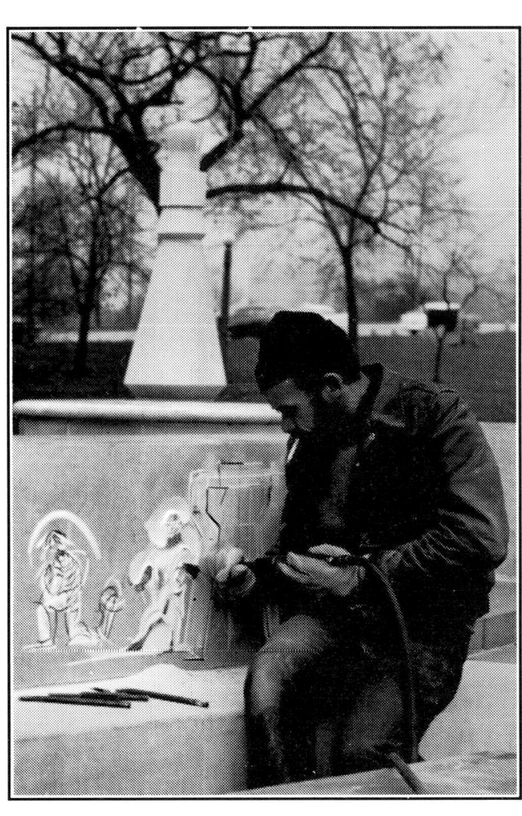

Gilbertson working on Chess Pavilion limestone relief, width 35', and one of two standing figures 48'' (1957)

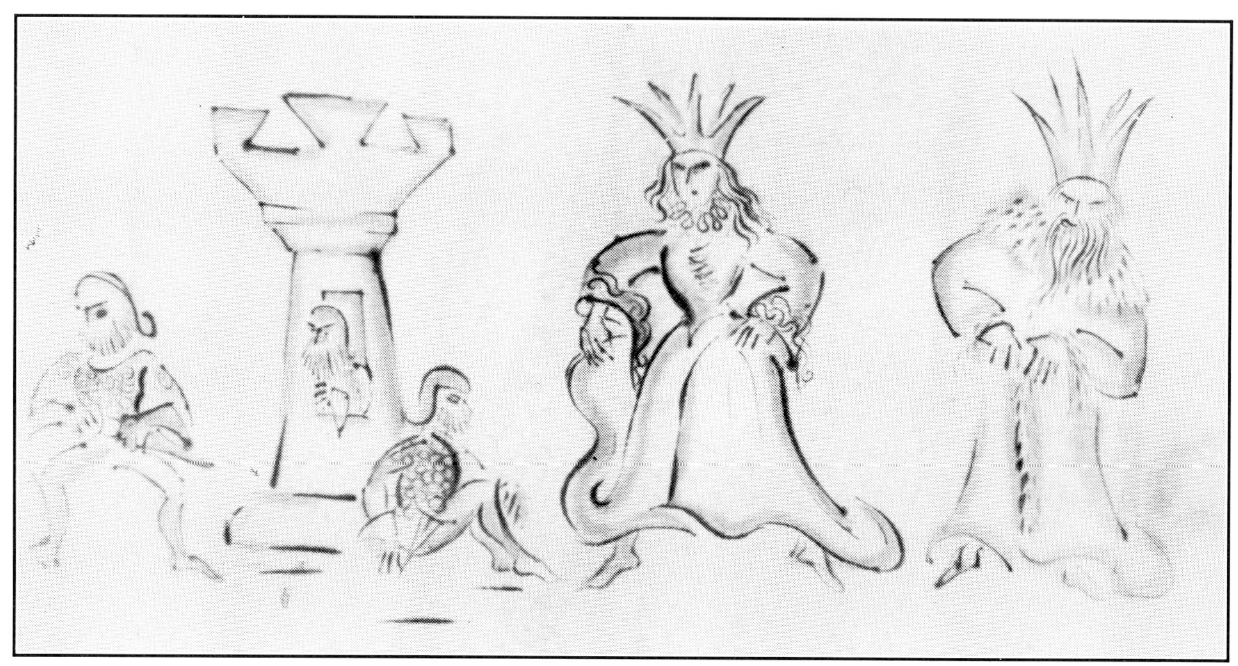

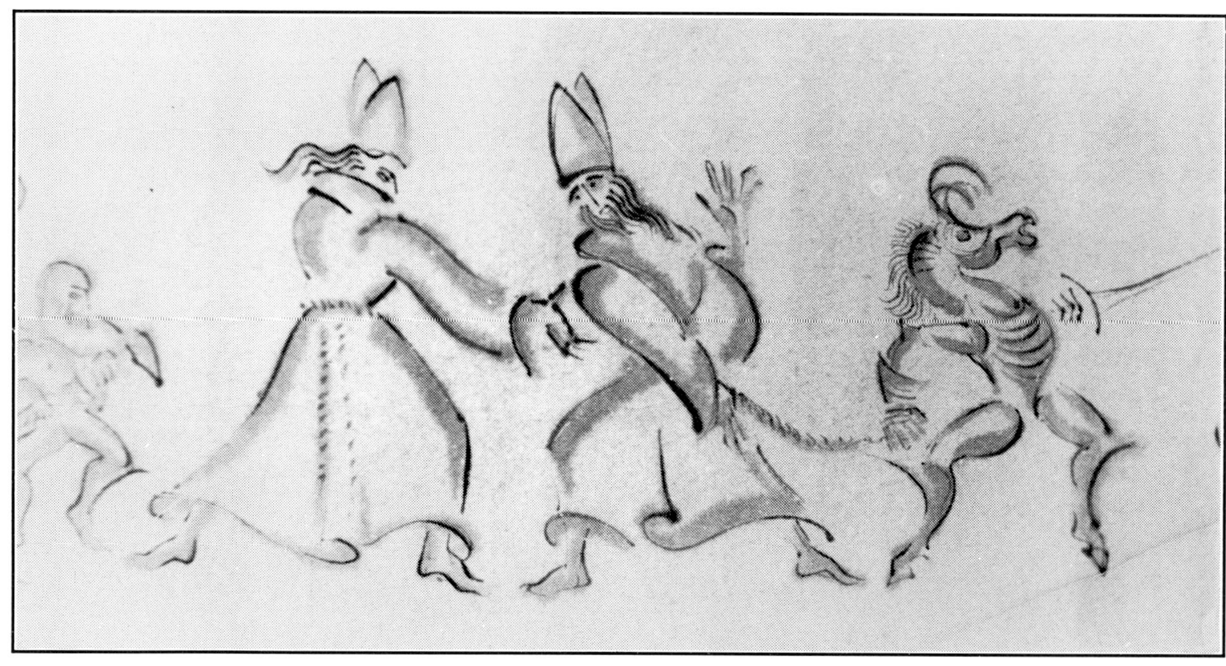

Drawings for Chess Pavilion carving,
Lincoln Park, Chicago

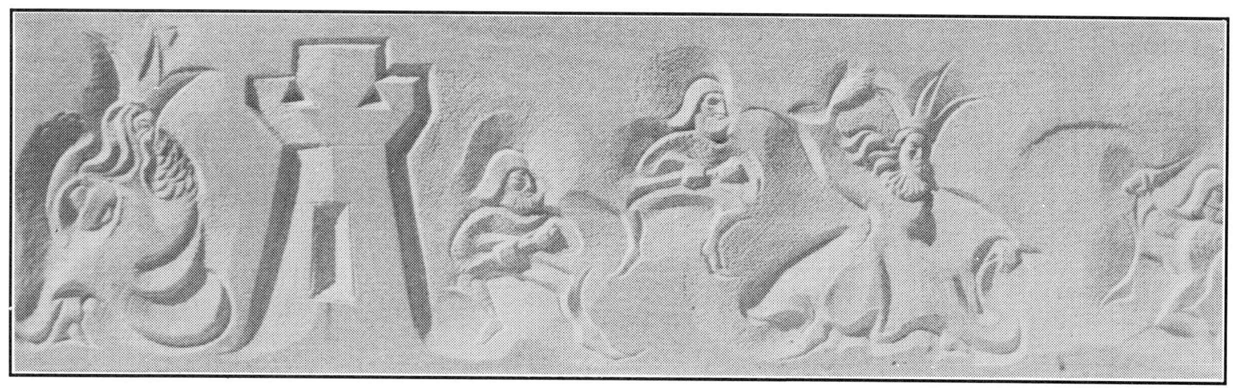

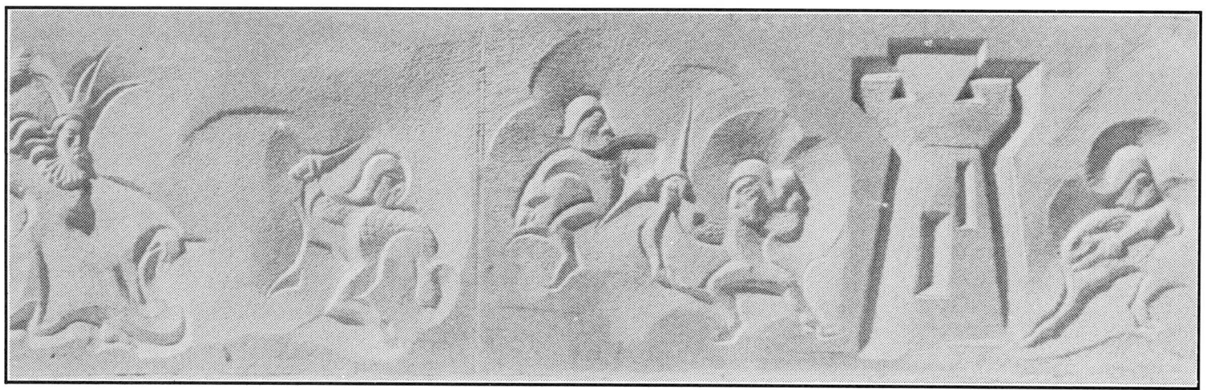

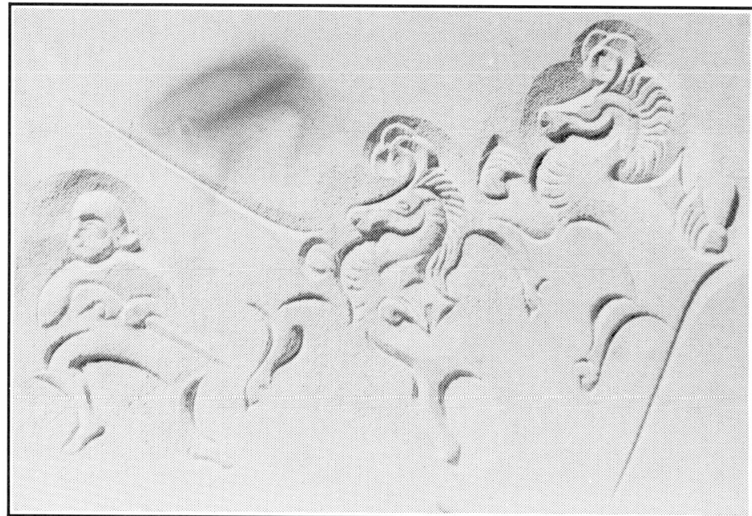

Detail of Chess Pavilion relief,
Lincoln Park, Chicago

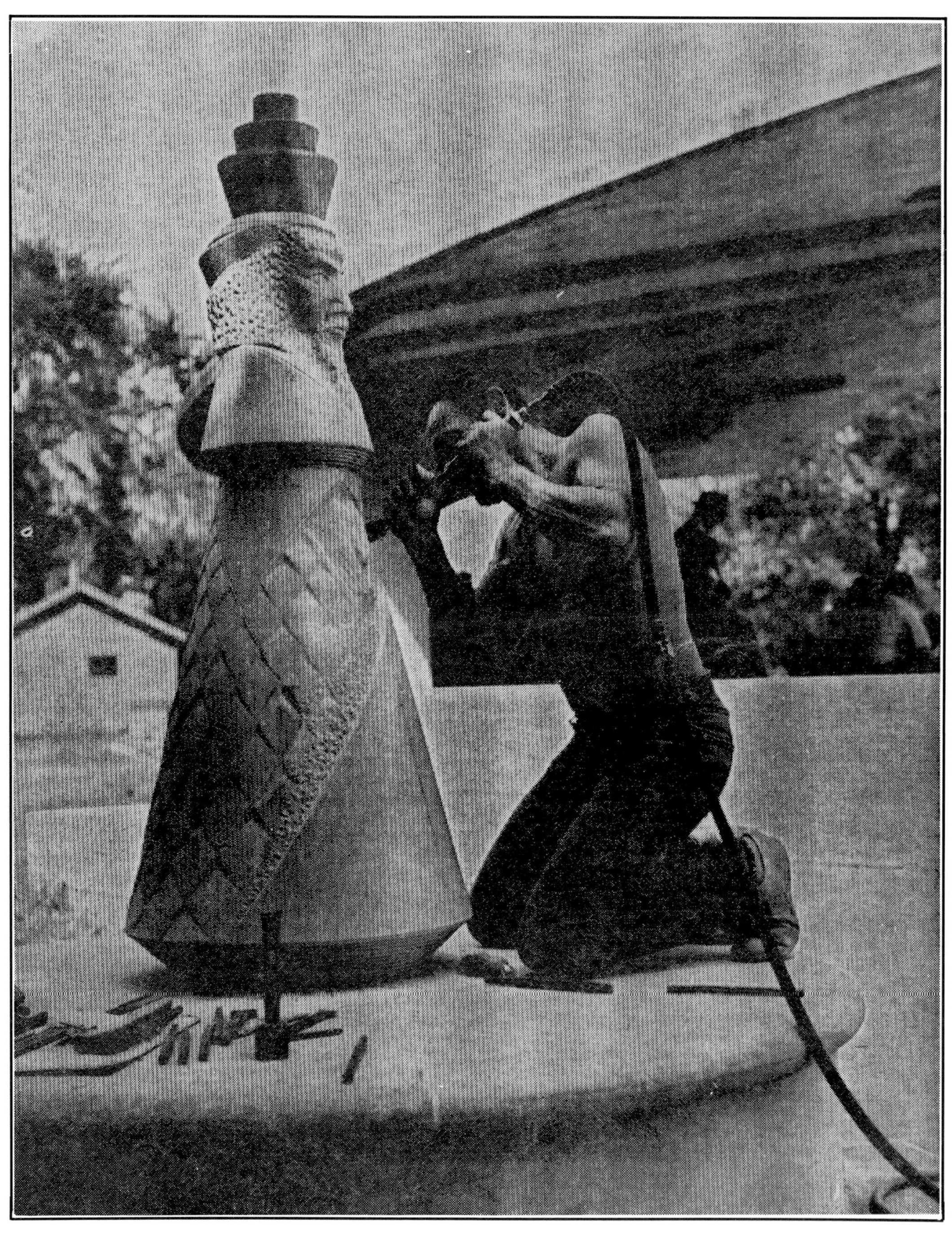

CHESS PAVILION KING, stone (1957) 48''

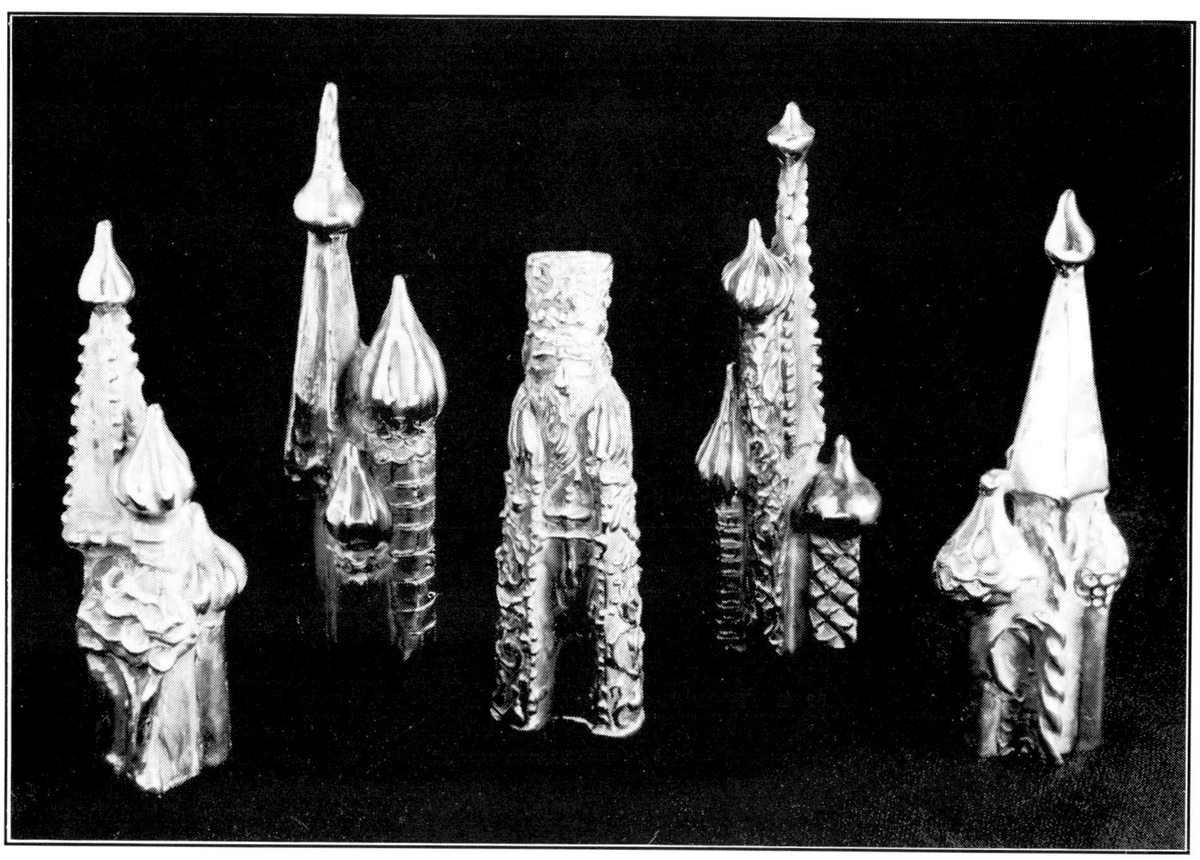

CHESS PIECES, cast bronze (1983) from wax models (1978) each 6″

Photo: Stephen Piersol

METAL

Gilbertson's metal sculptures were one of a kind, some very similar as variations on a theme. With one exception, he cast none of his work, believing that in that process the artist lost contact with the work, creating something comparable to a print of a painting.

He worked with his torch, building drop by drop of molten metal. First making a rough shape of what he had in mind from sheet copper, he built slowly, painstakingly, then ground the piece to shape; hours of polishing followed.

He made all his own bases to suit each subject, spending days on these alone. He collected many kinds of wood, including juniper roots and driftwood, and rocks—lava rocks were favorites. He would burn, polish, chip, and shape until they too suited him.

The small pieces are solid metal, silver or bronze; Gilbertson used his torch as he did his Chinese brushes, as though he were drawing. For creatures with spots or stripes, he would use silver or burn in holes or lines with his torch.

He preferred using animals in his work, for he said: ''Then any feeling can be evoked, just as in Russian fables or as in 'The Wind in the Willows'.''

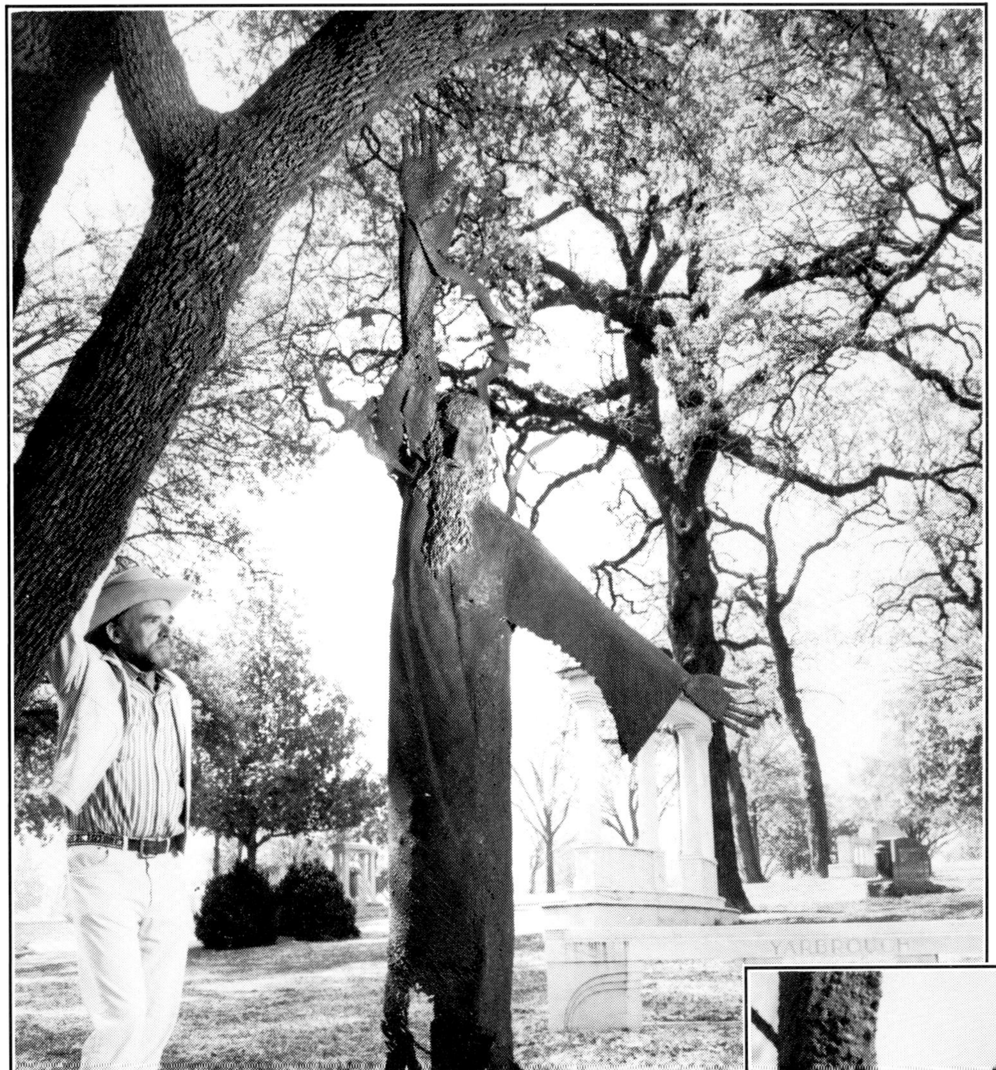

Gilbertson with ELIJAH in place
at Fort Worth, Texas. Bronze and
corten steel (1971) 16'

Detail of ELIJAH

30

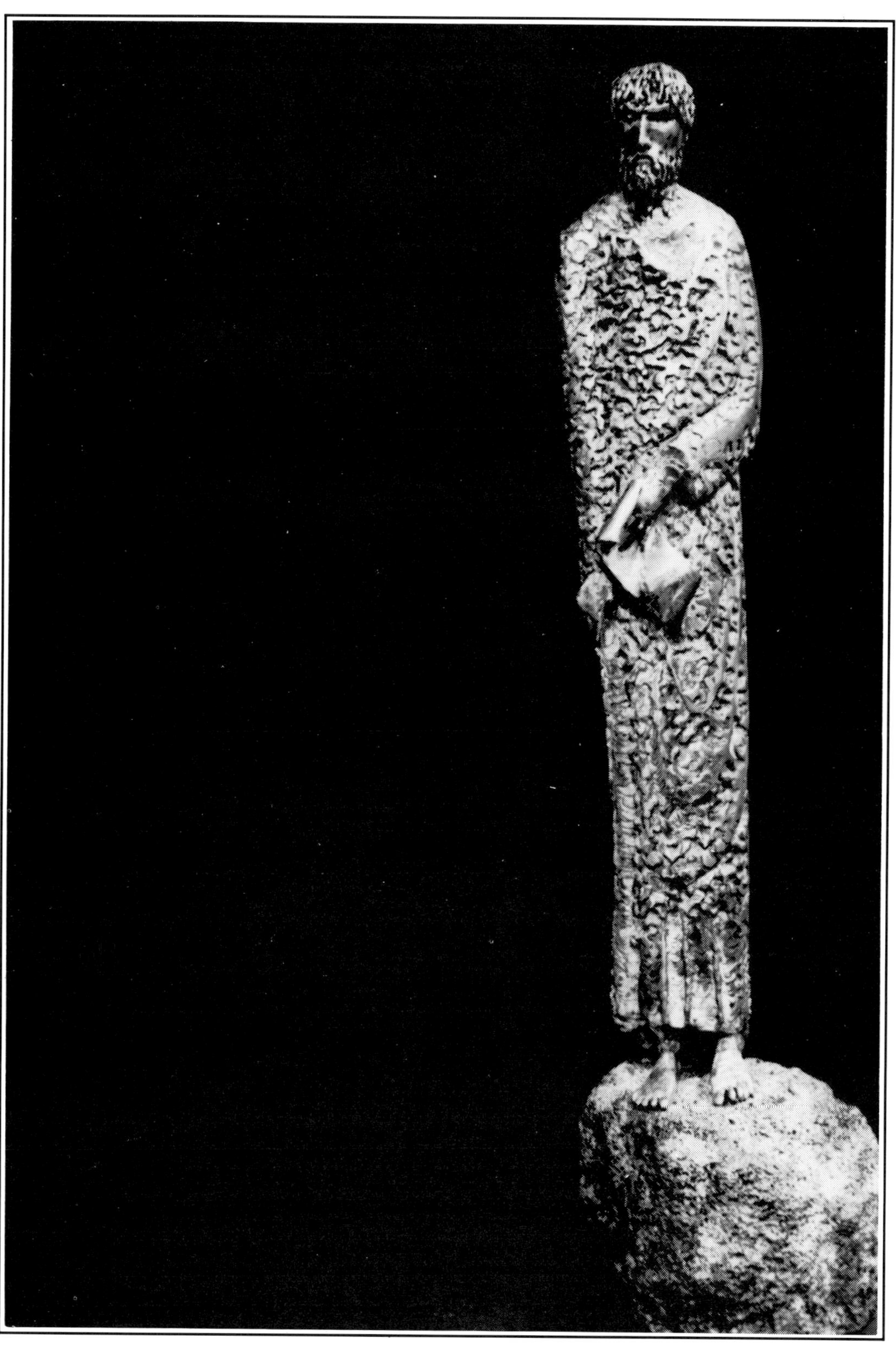

PROPHET, bronze (1965) 18''

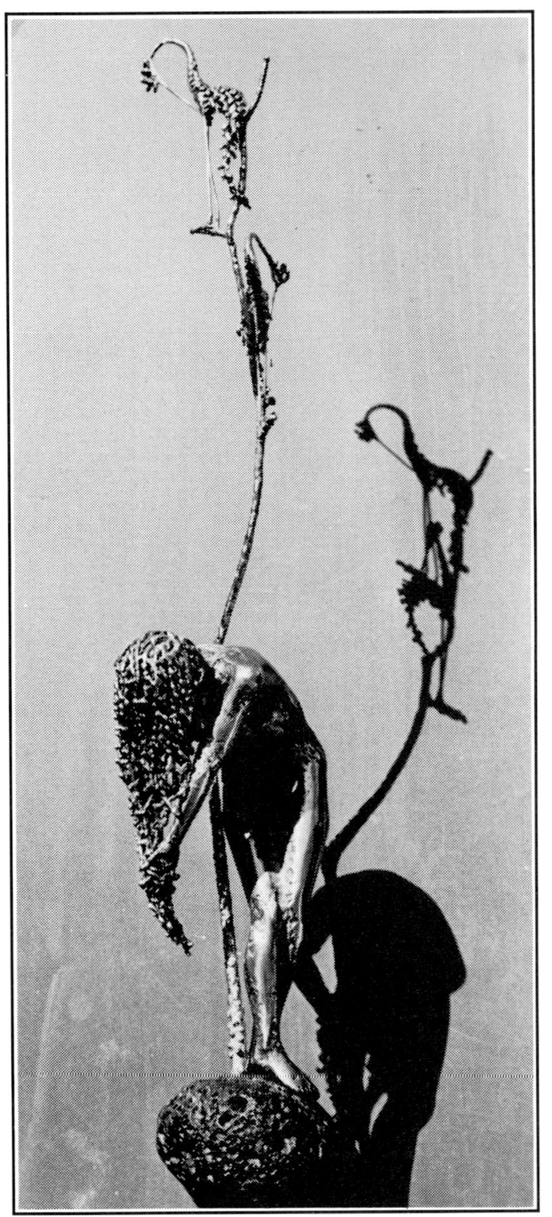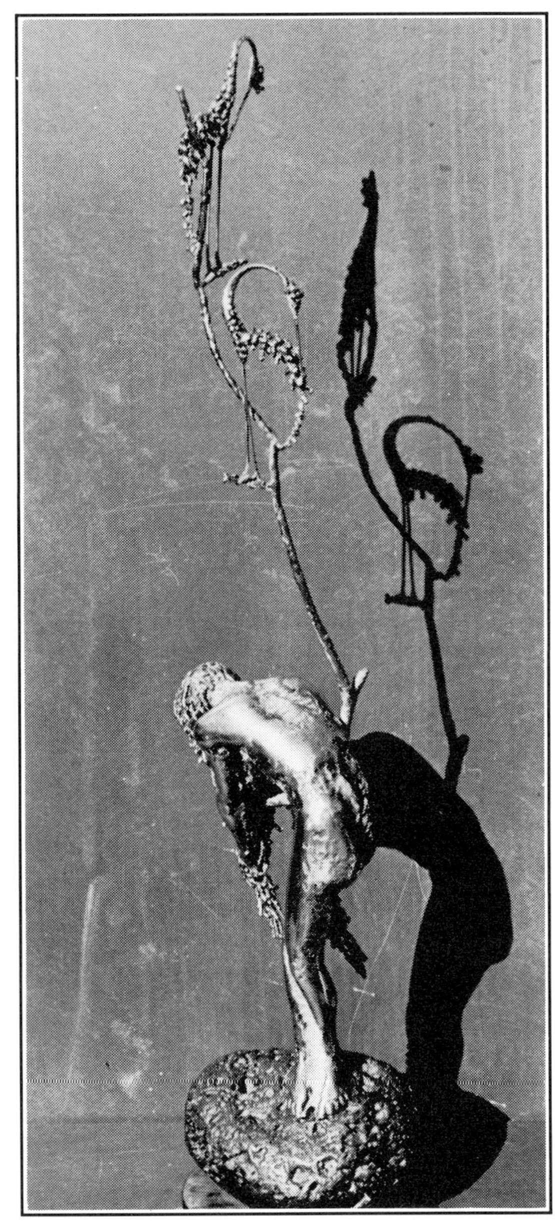

BIRDS OF A FEATHER, bronze (1967) 21″ Photo: Karl Kernberger

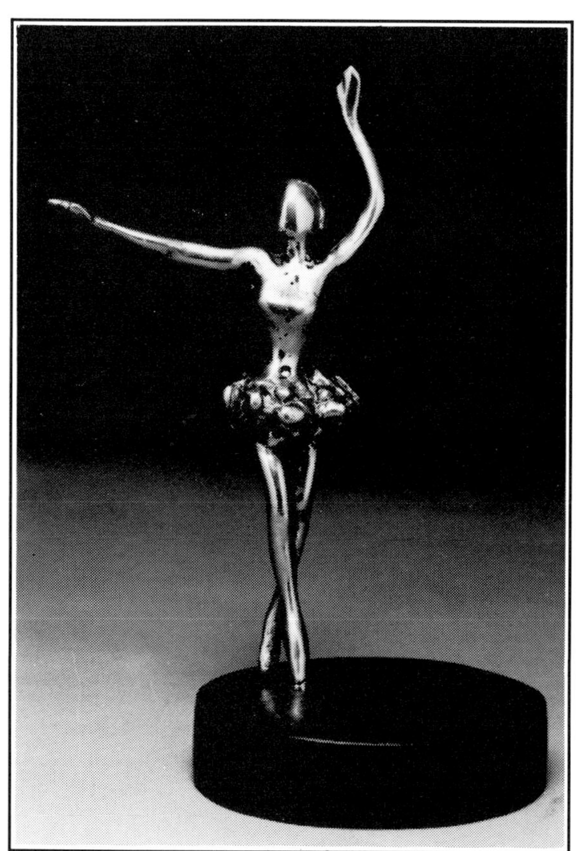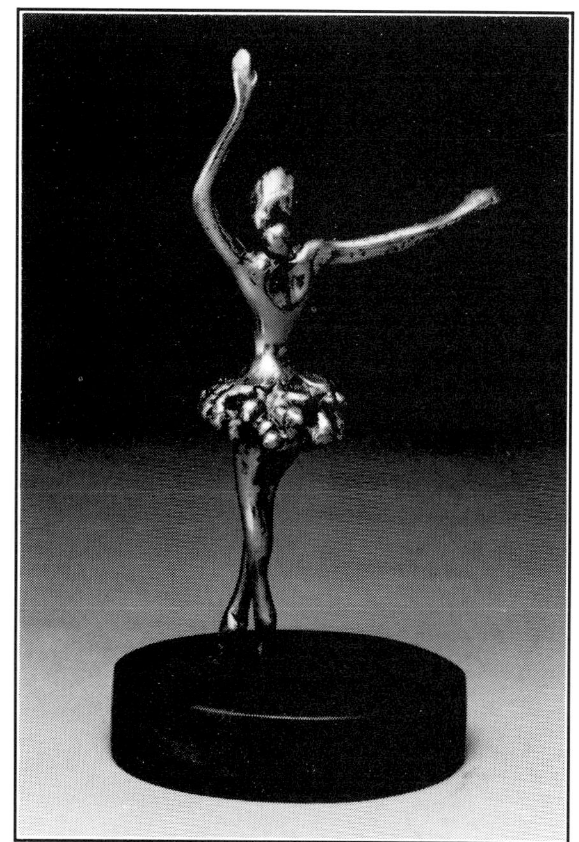

BALLERINA, bronze (1968) 6½''

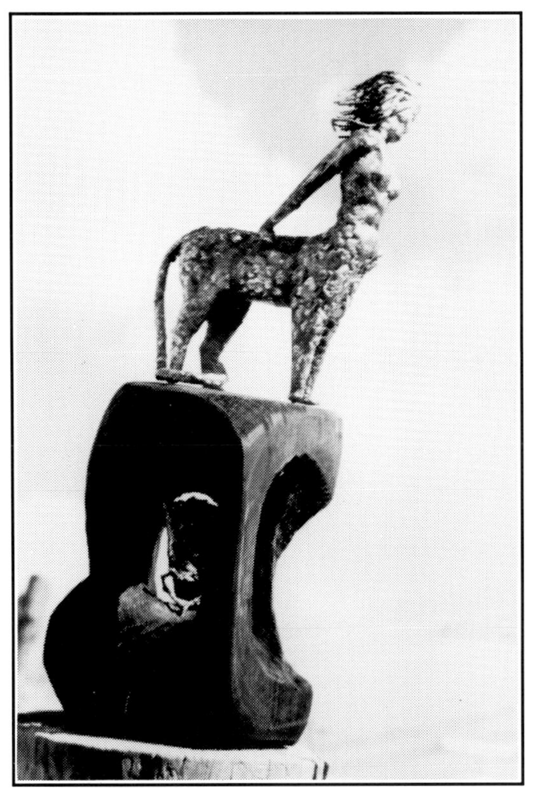

CATAUR, bronze (1962) 8½'' x 11½''

NUDE/PARROT, bronze (1962) 10''

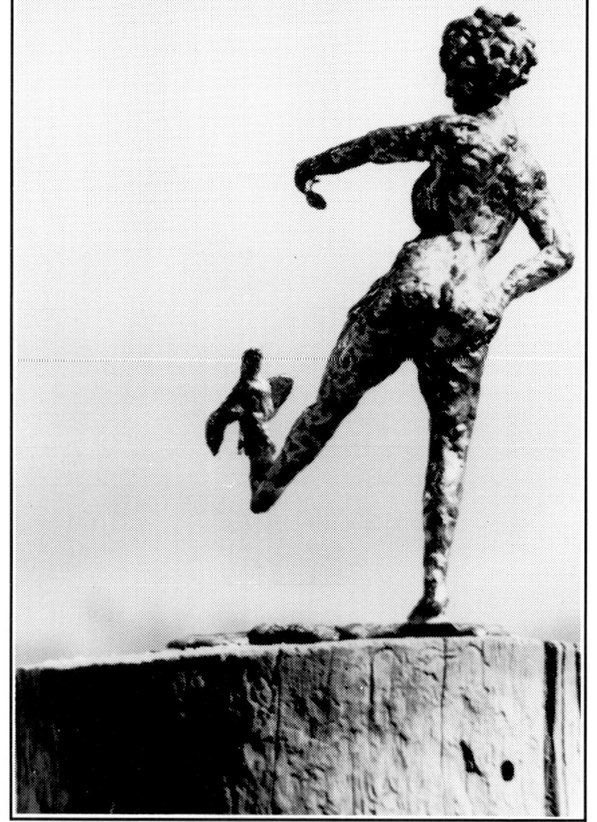

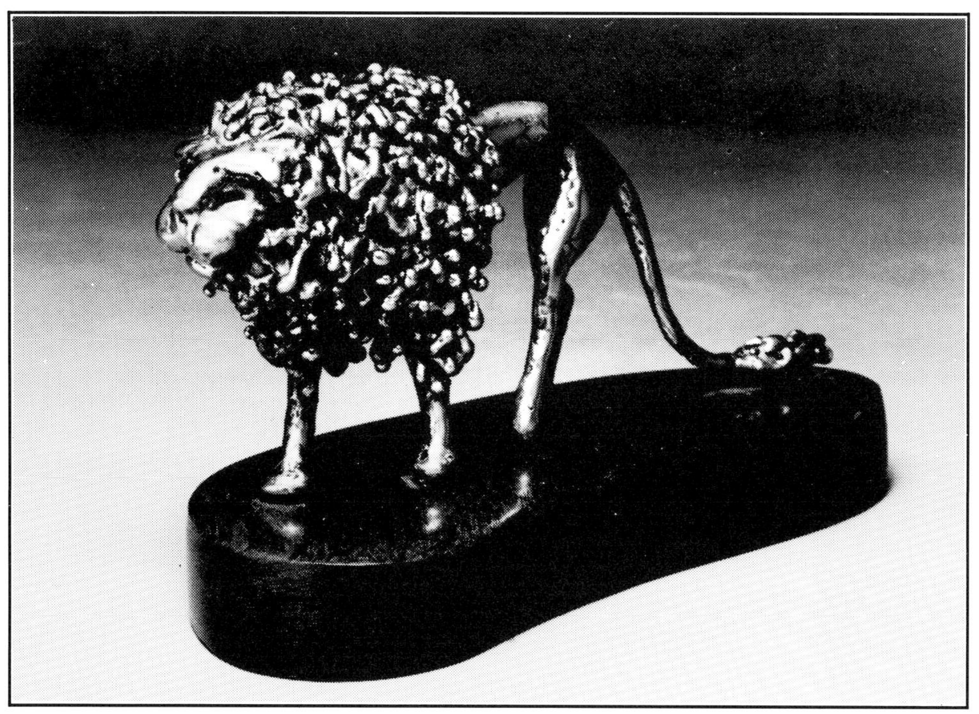

LION, bronze (1970) 3½'' x 7½''

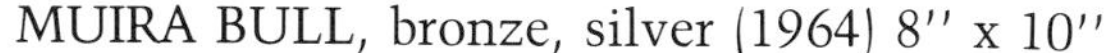

MUIRA BULL, bronze, silver (1964) 8'' x 10''

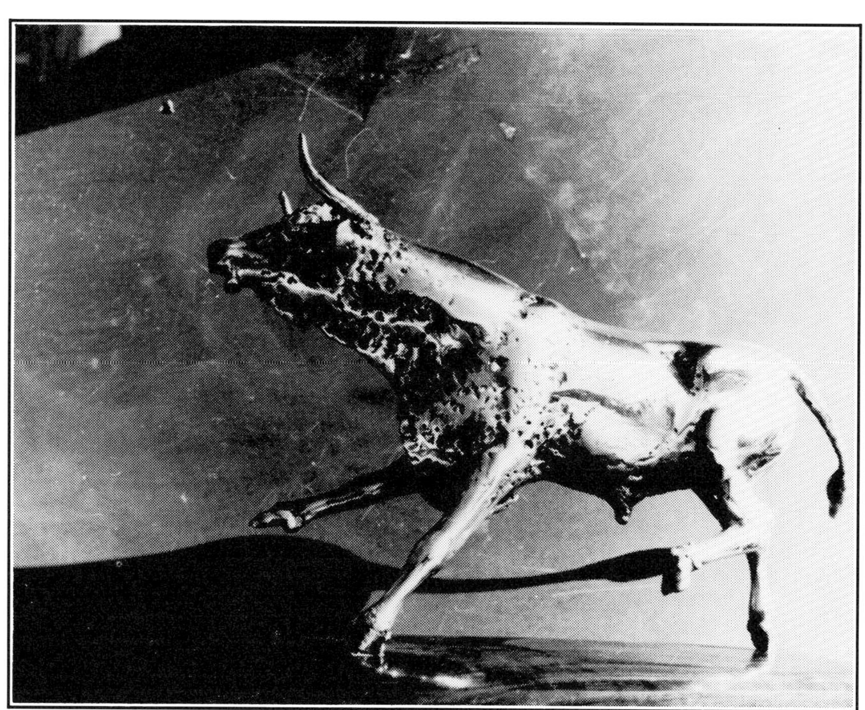

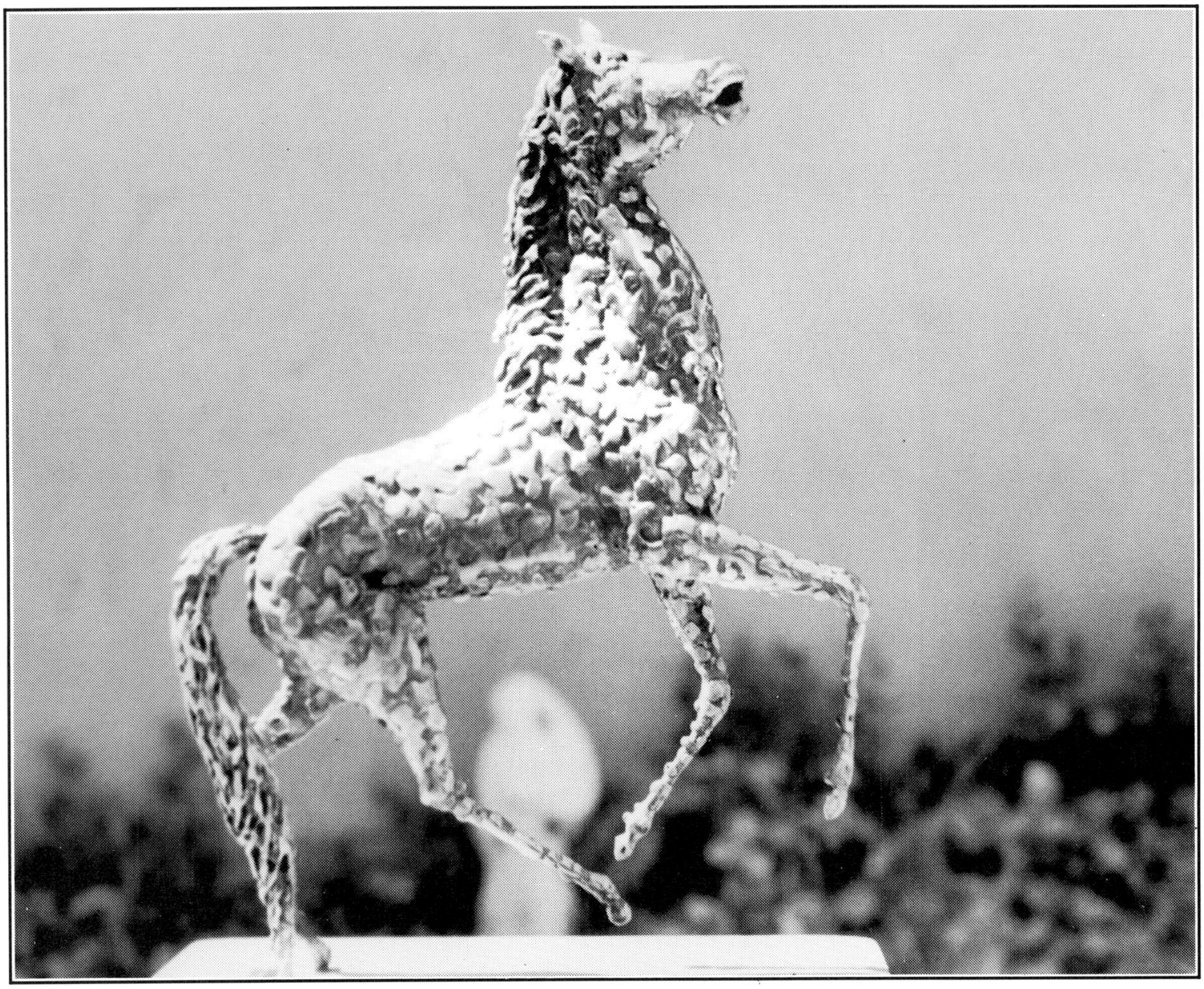

PRANCING HORSE, bronze (1970) 10'' x 8''

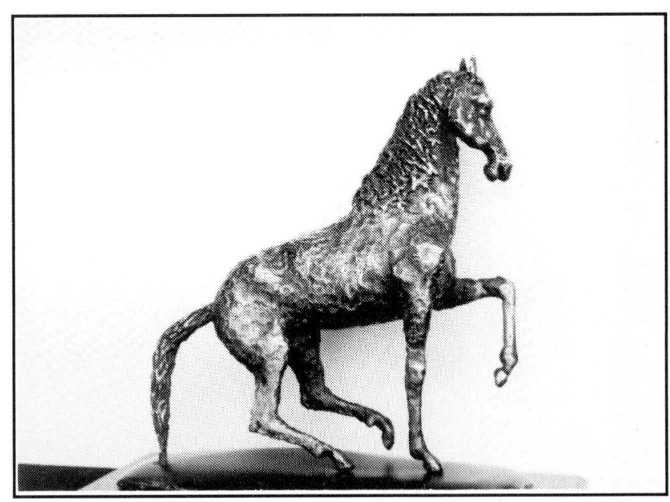

HORSE, bronze (1979) 14'' x 14''

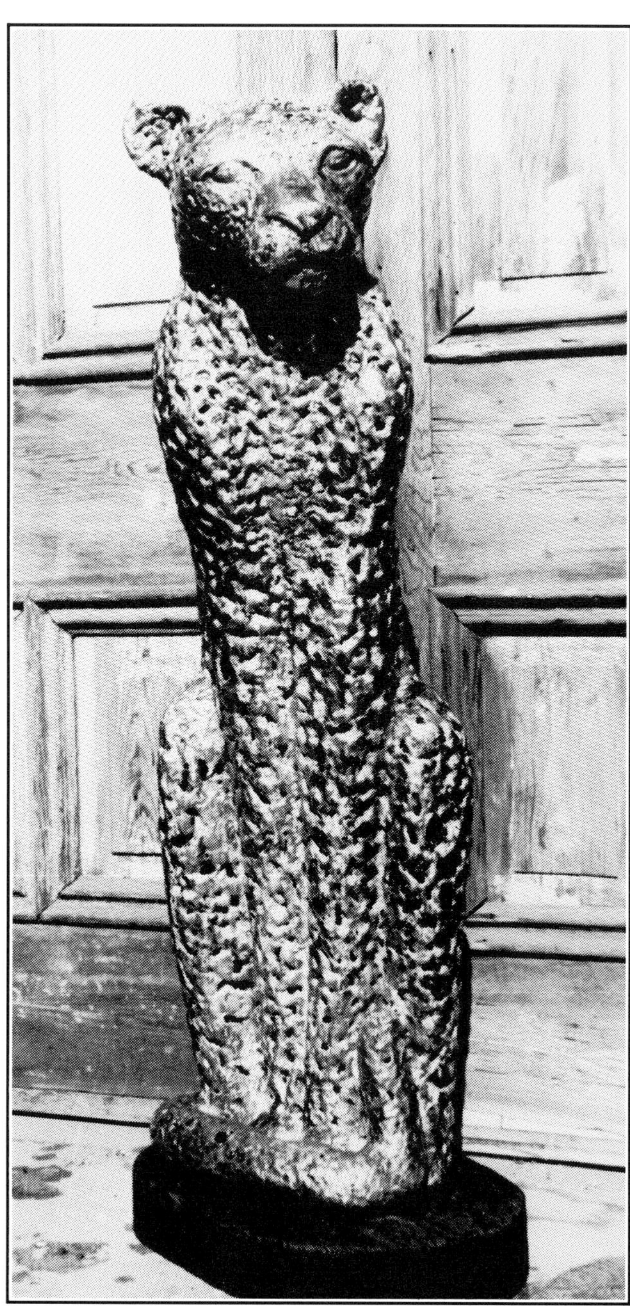

JAGUAR, bronze, burned spots (1968) 42''

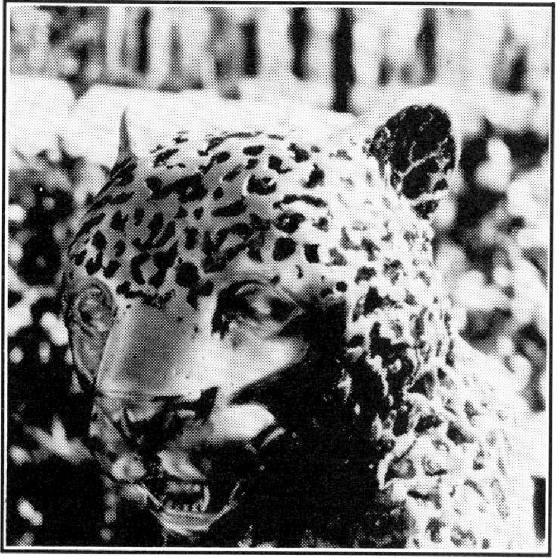

Detail of JAGUAR

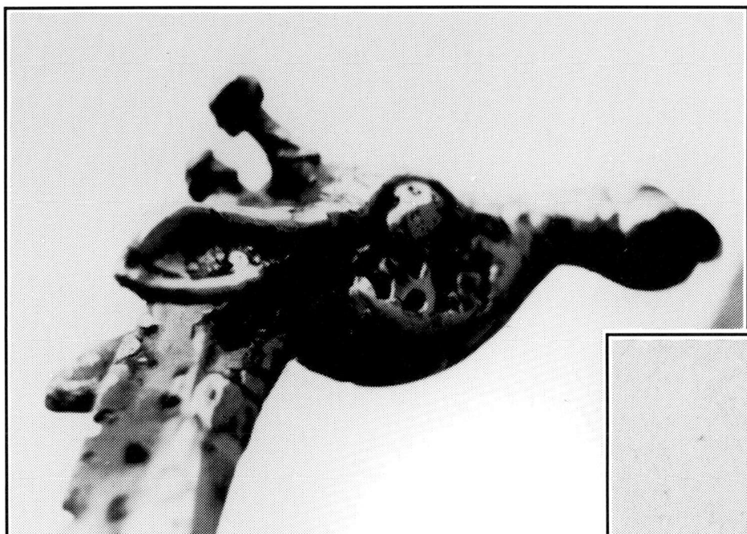

Detail of GIRAFFE

GIRAFFE, bronze,
coin silver spots (1965) 33″

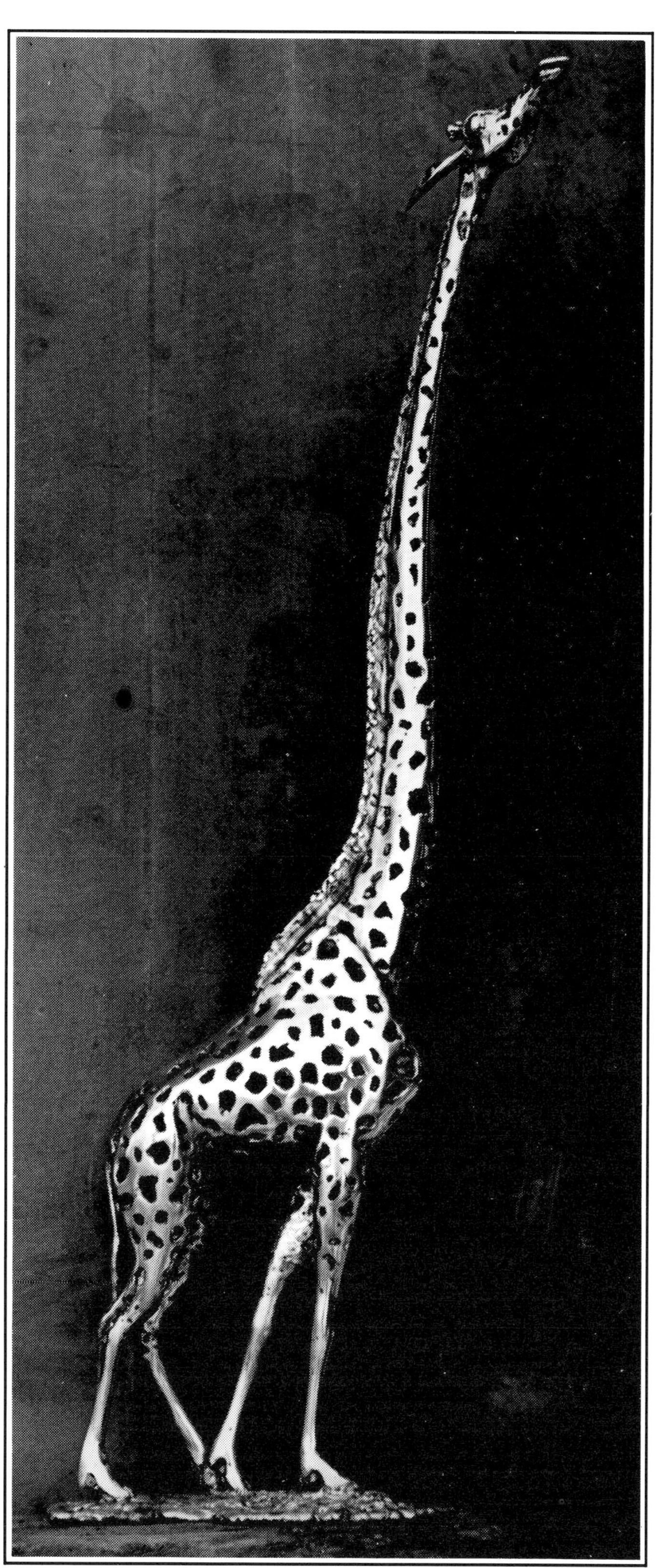

GIRAFFE, bronze,
burned spots (1965) 36''

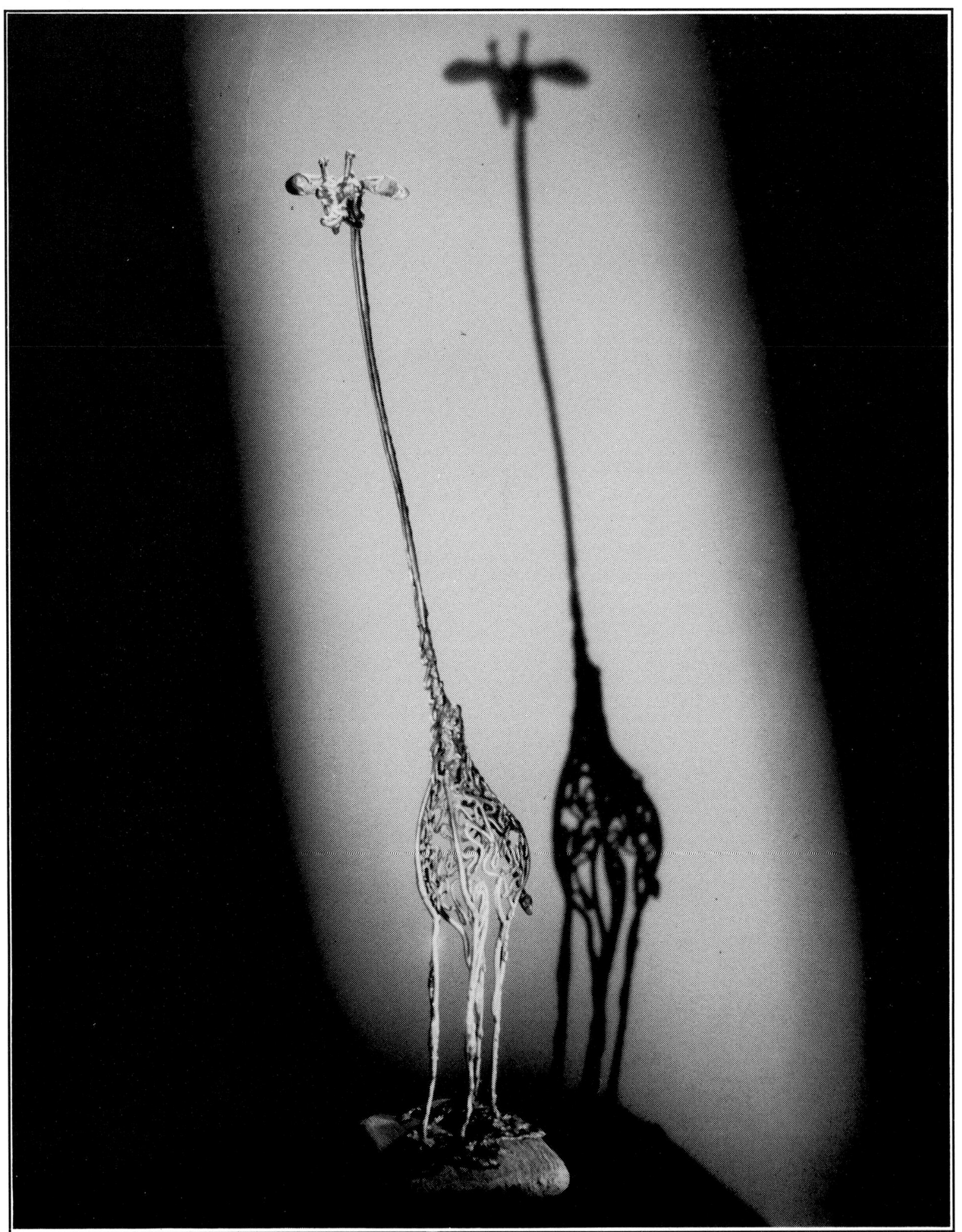

GIRAFFE, bronze, filigree (1972) 31'' Photo, MILO

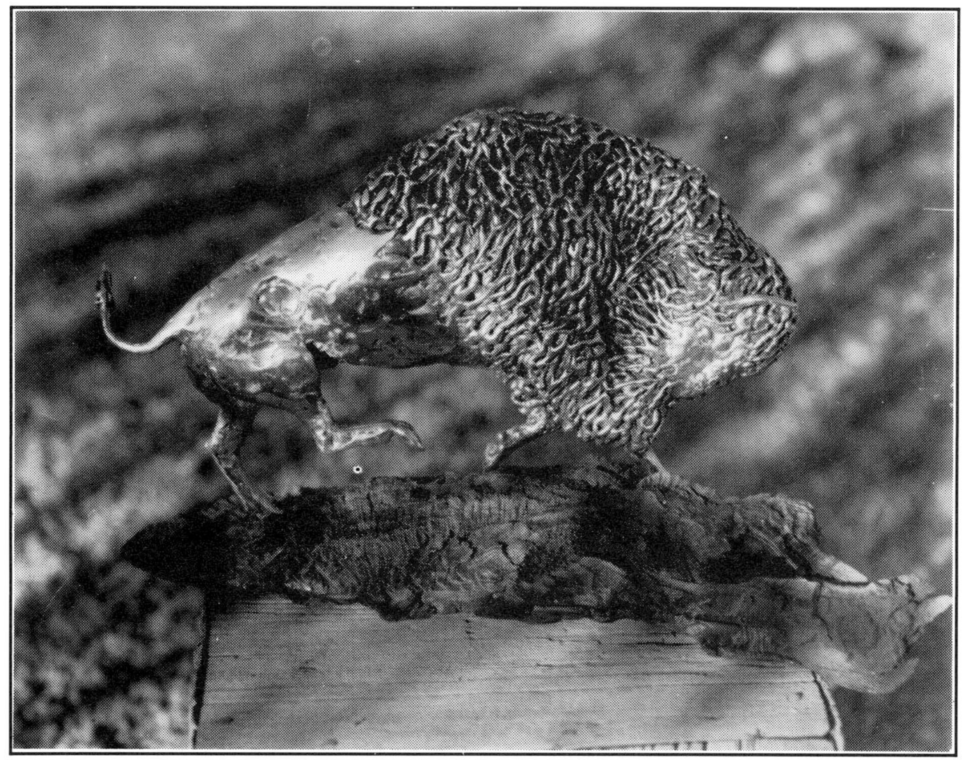

BISON, bronze (1972) 5'' x 10''

TIGER, bronze, burned stripes (1964) 5'' x 11''

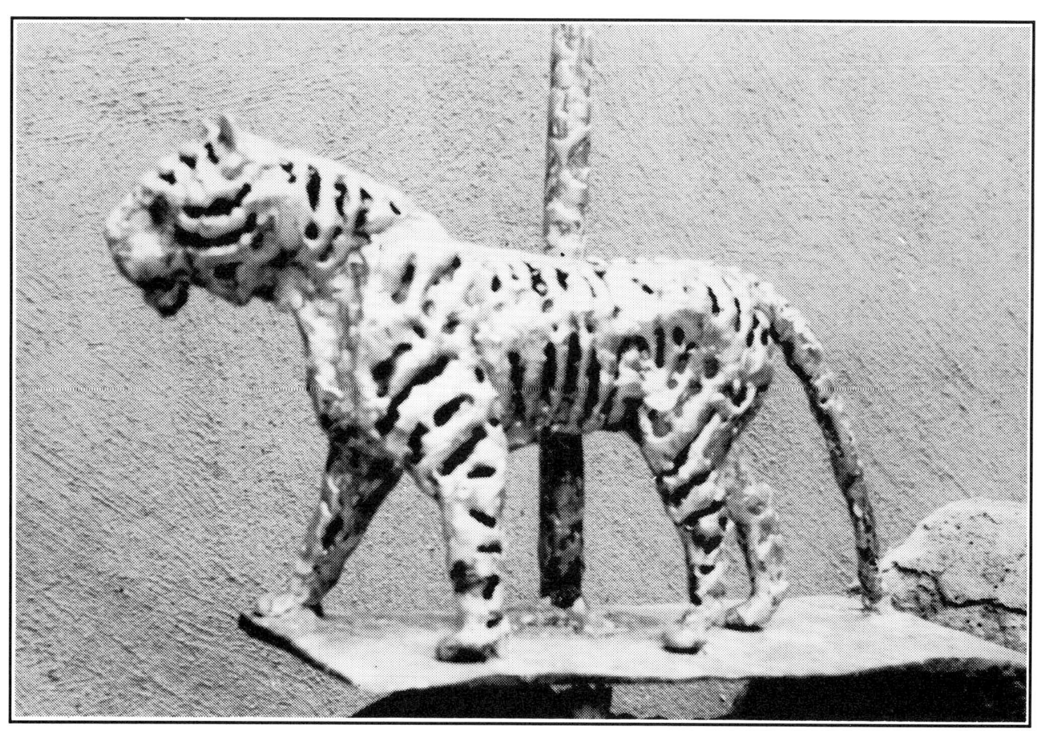

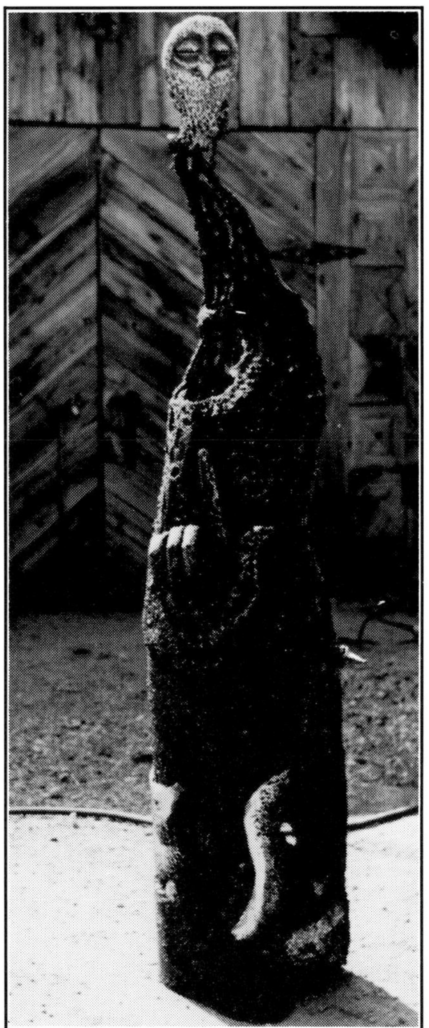

ODE TO BEATRIX POTTER, corten steel, bronze (1974) 7'

Detail, ODE TO BEATRIX POTTER

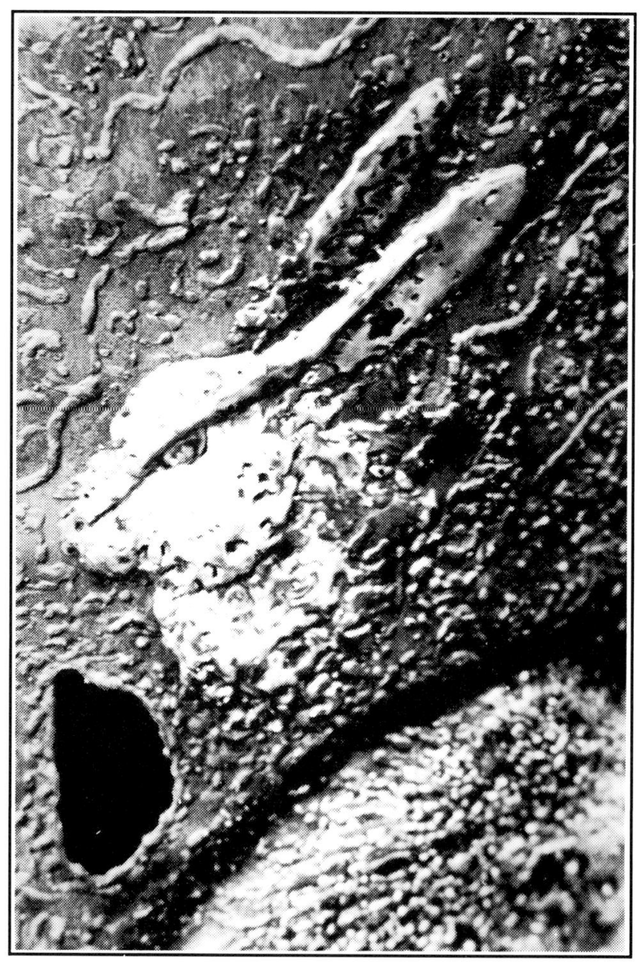

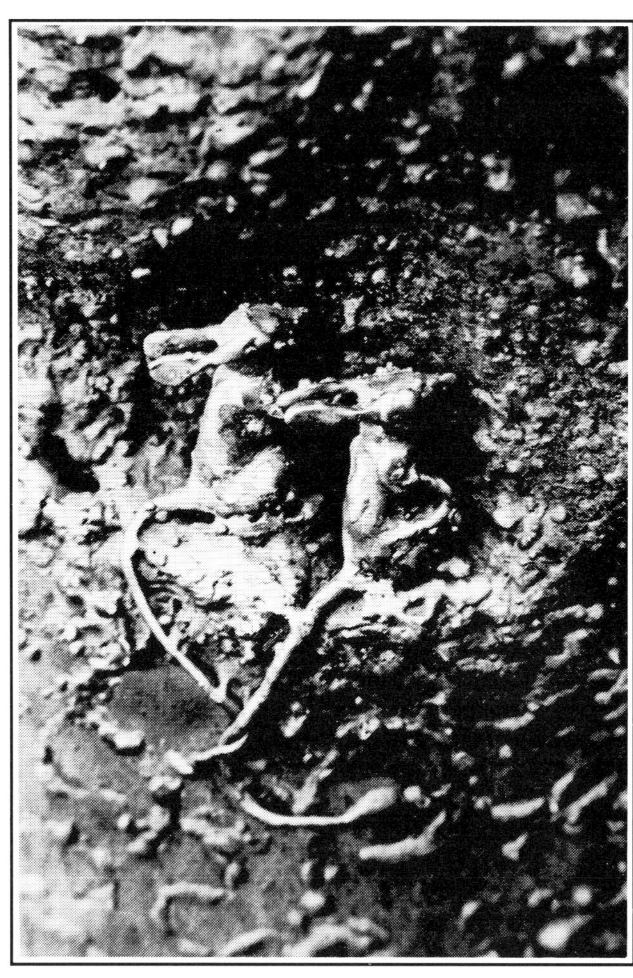

Detail, ODE TO BEATRIX POTTER

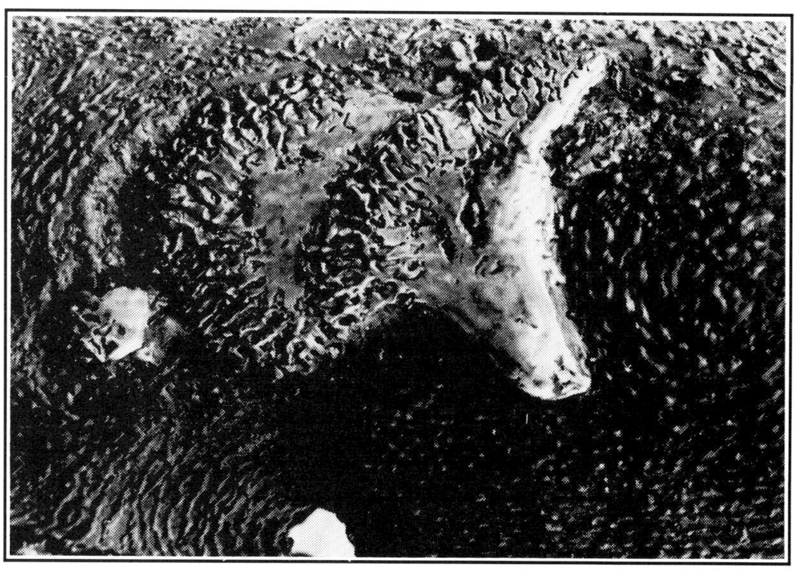

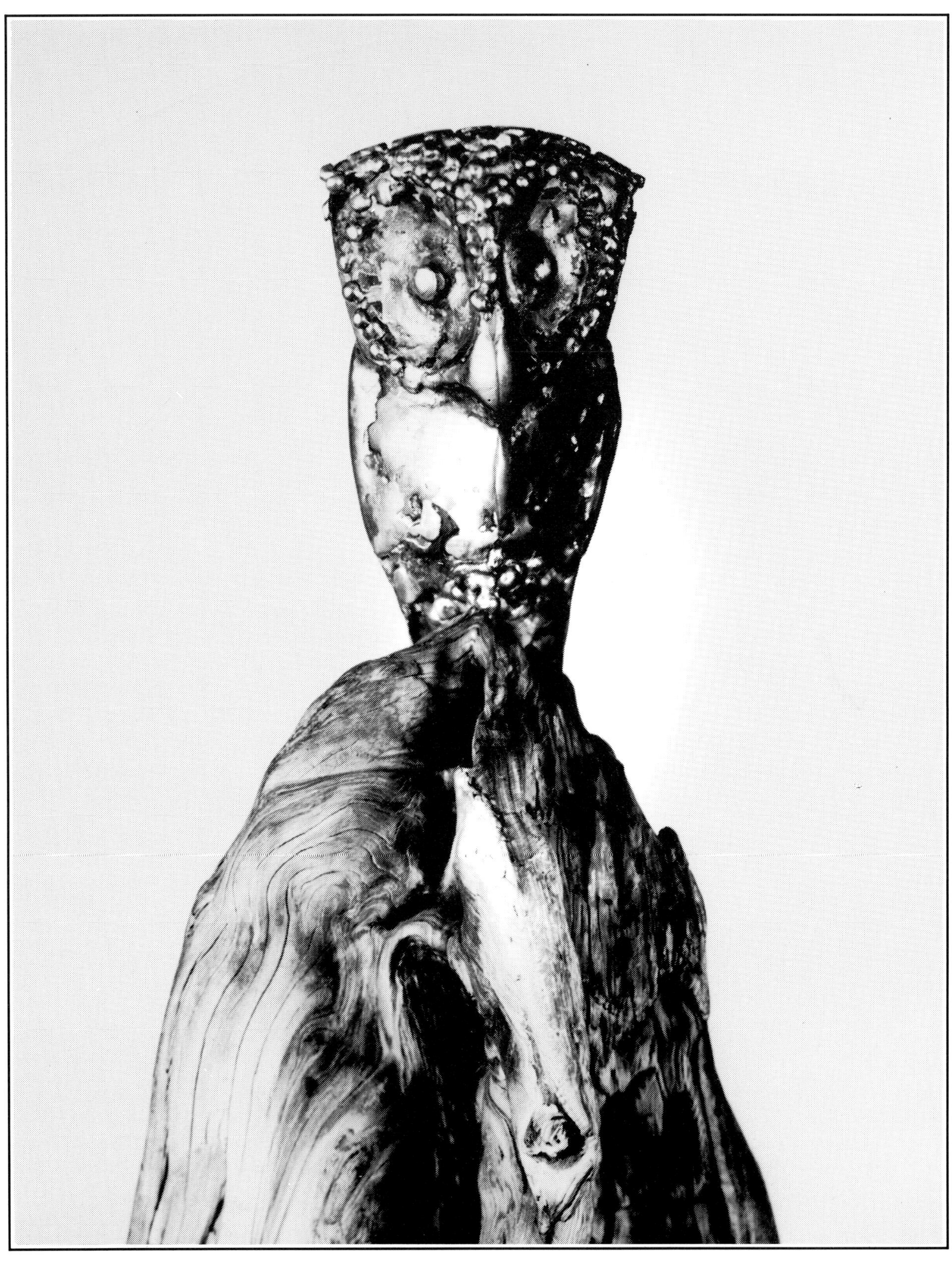

OWL ON CEDAR ROOT, bronze, (1966) 8''

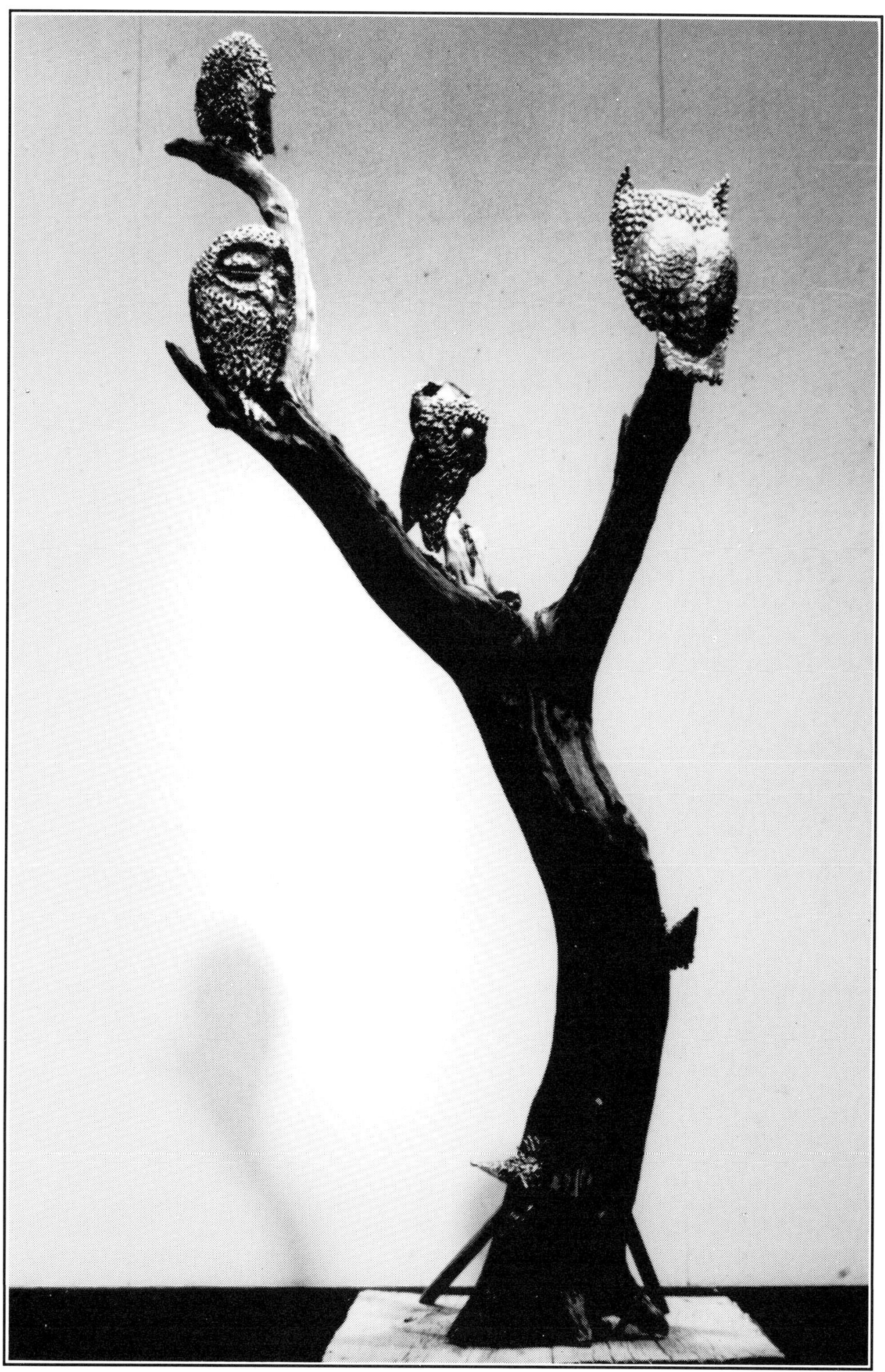

FAMILY TREE, bronze (1967) 6½'

OWL, bronze (1963) 10''

OWL #2, bronze (1968) 8''

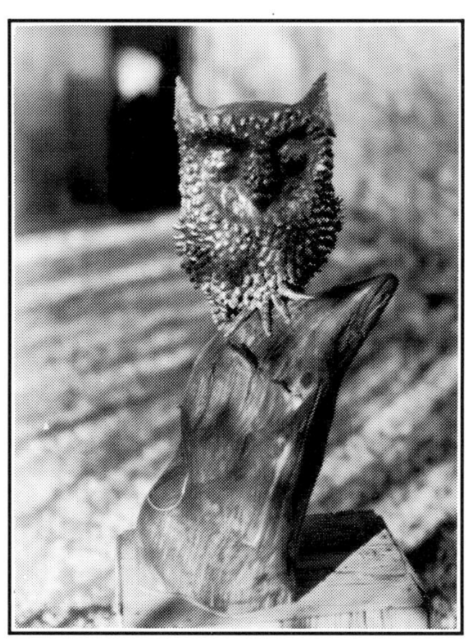

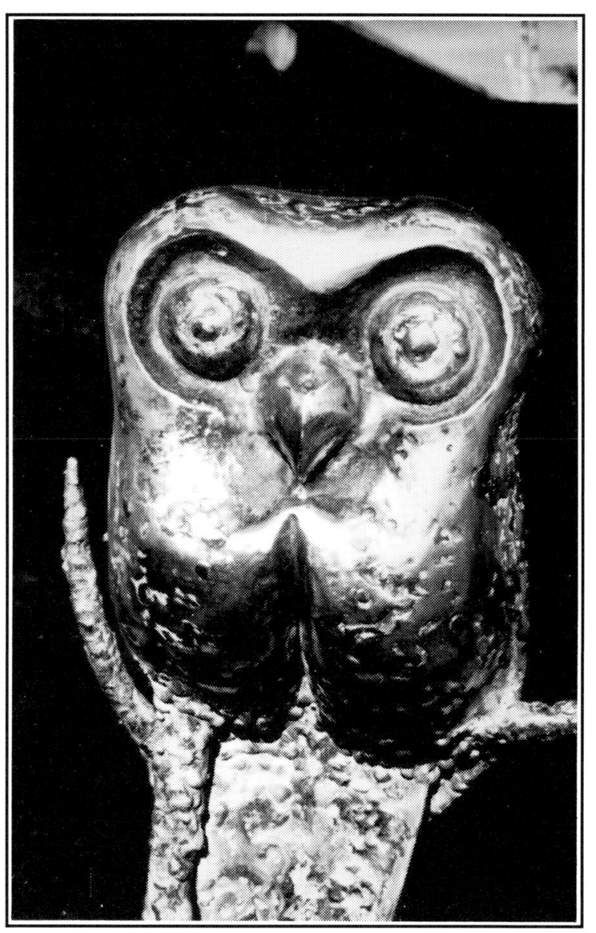

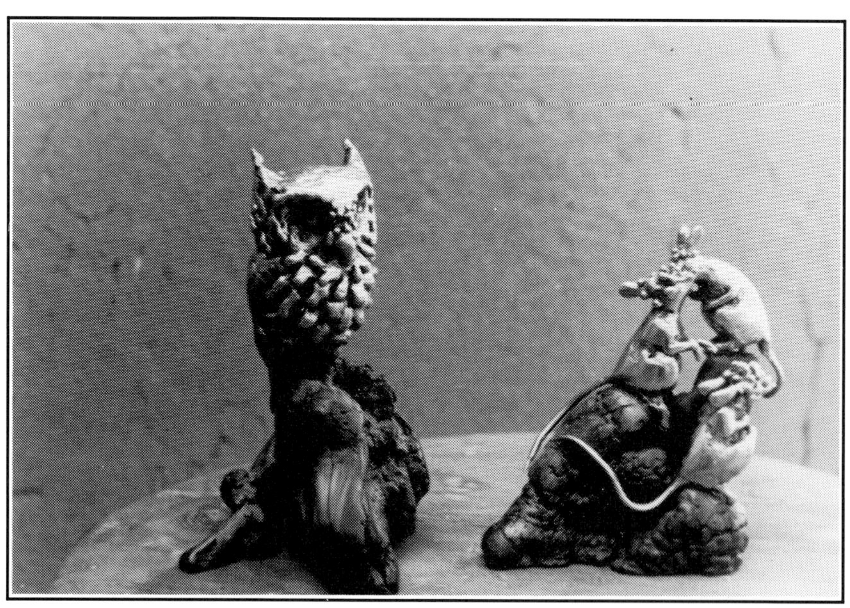

THREE'S A CROWD, bronze (1964) Owl 4½'', Mice (each) 2½''

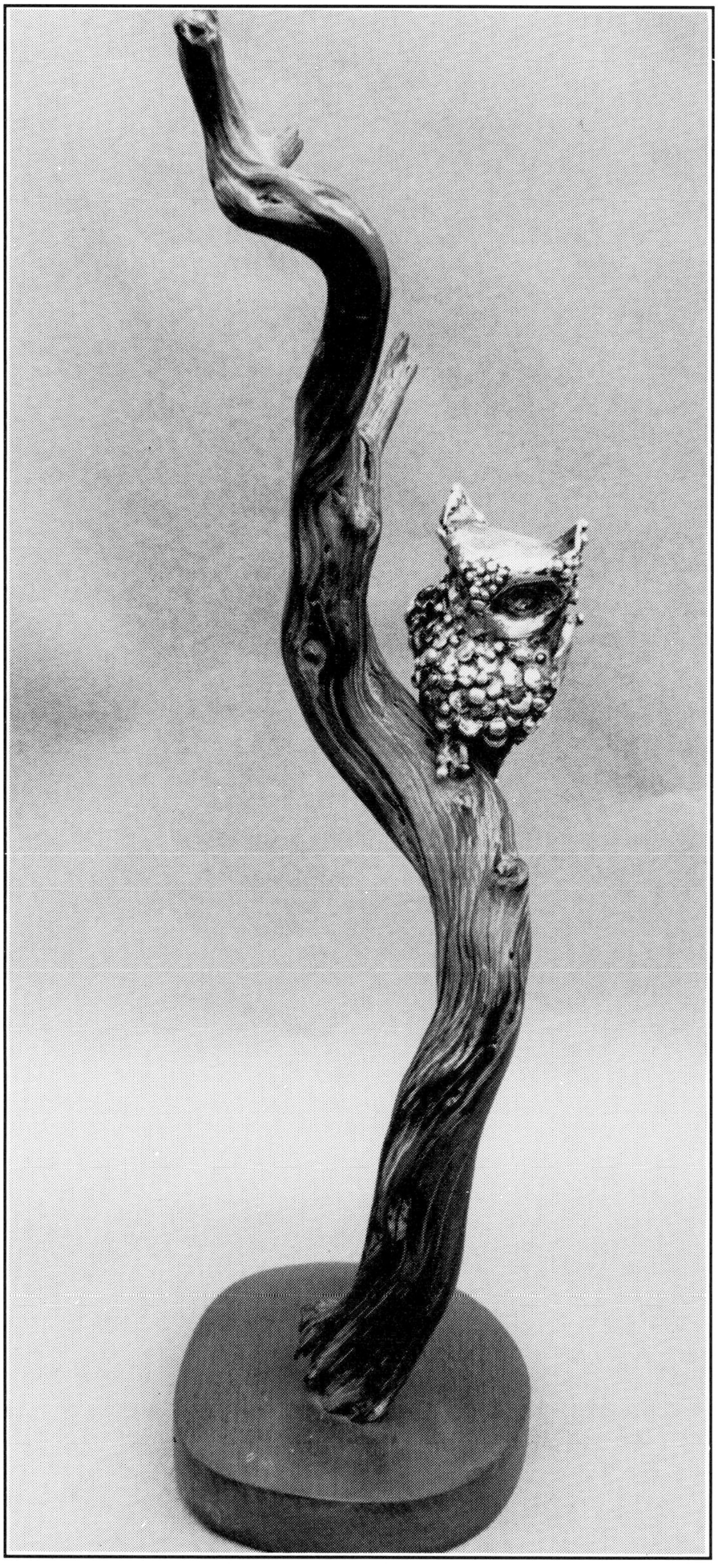

OWL ON DRIFTWOOD, silver (1972) owl 4''

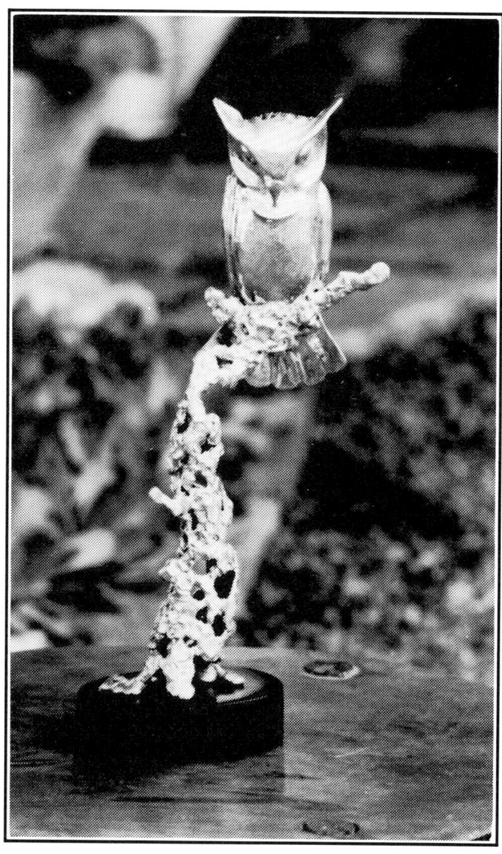

OWL ON BRANCH, fine silver (1979) 8''

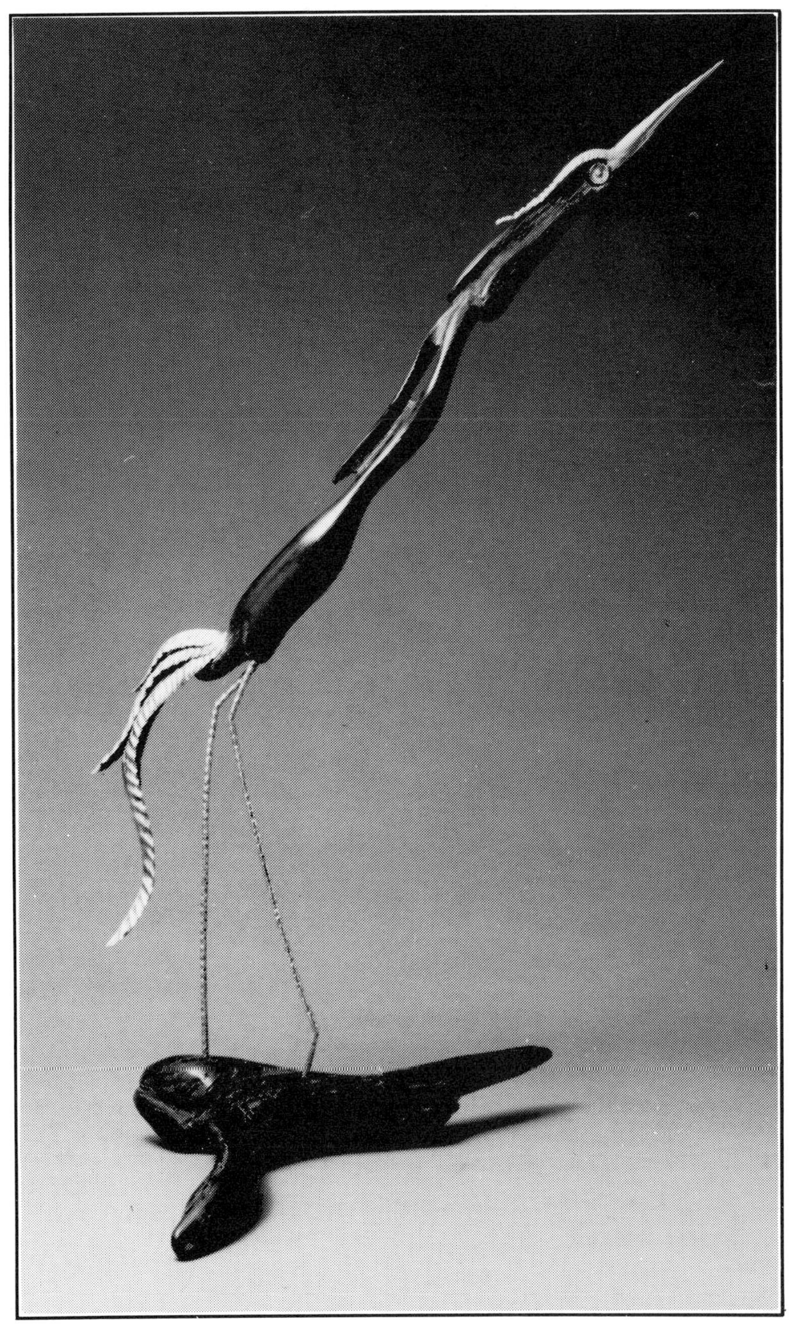

FIREBIRD, silver, ironwood (1980) 28″
Photo: Stephen Piersol

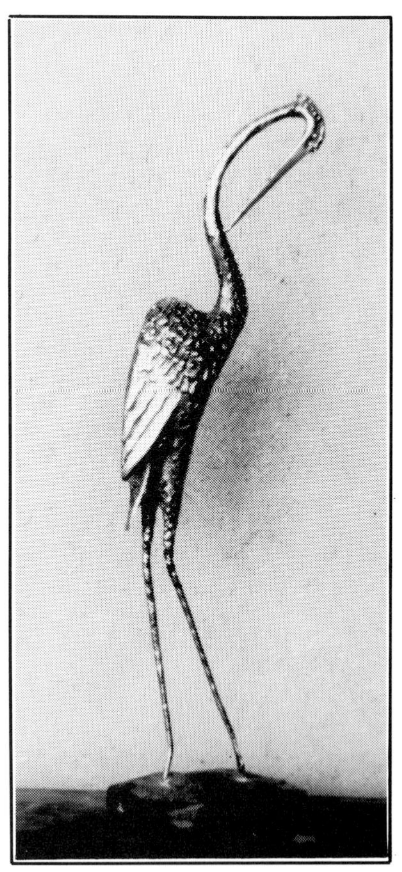

HERON, bronze (1950) 21″

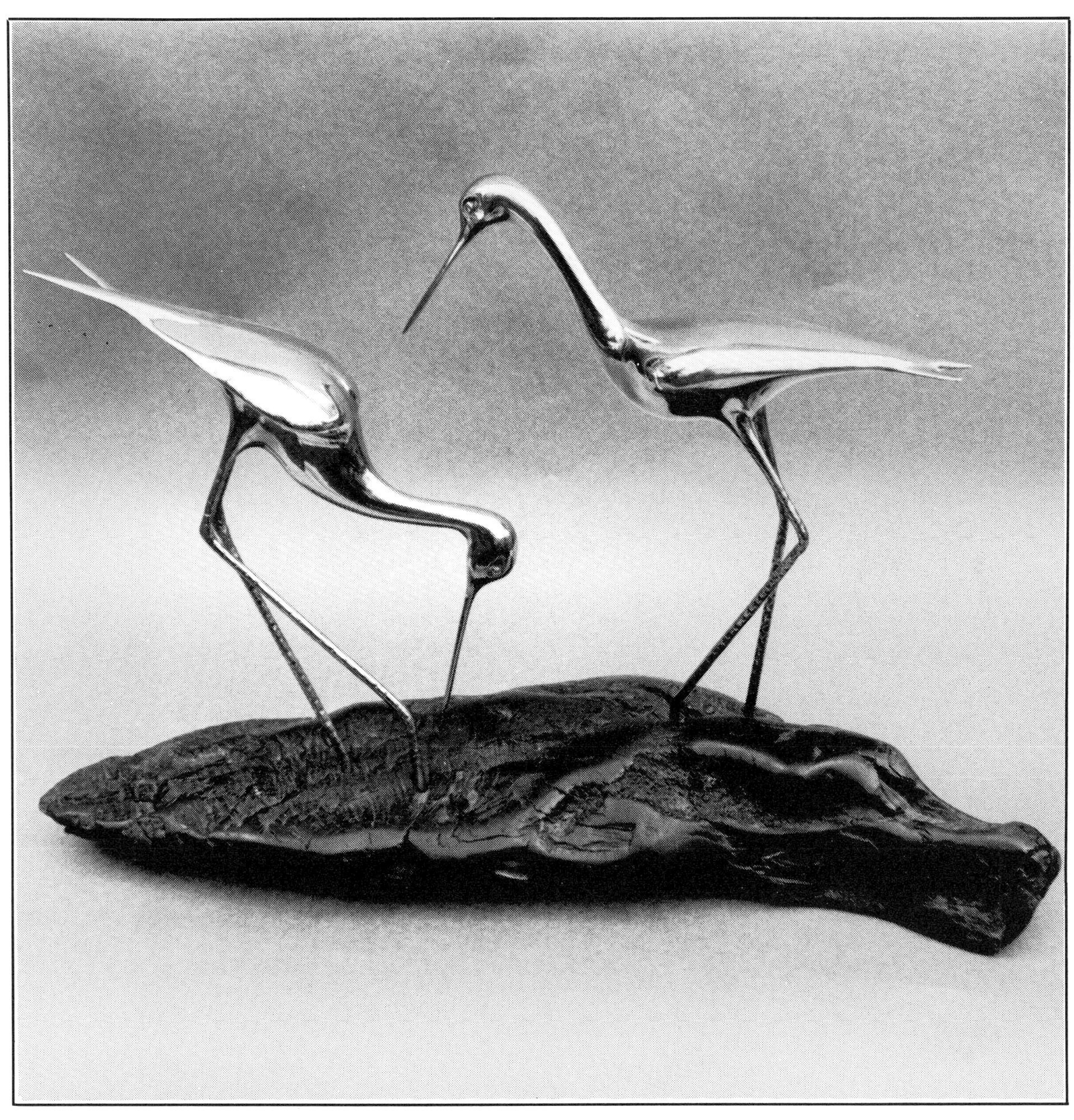

SHOREBIRDS, bronze (1972) 12'', width at base 19''

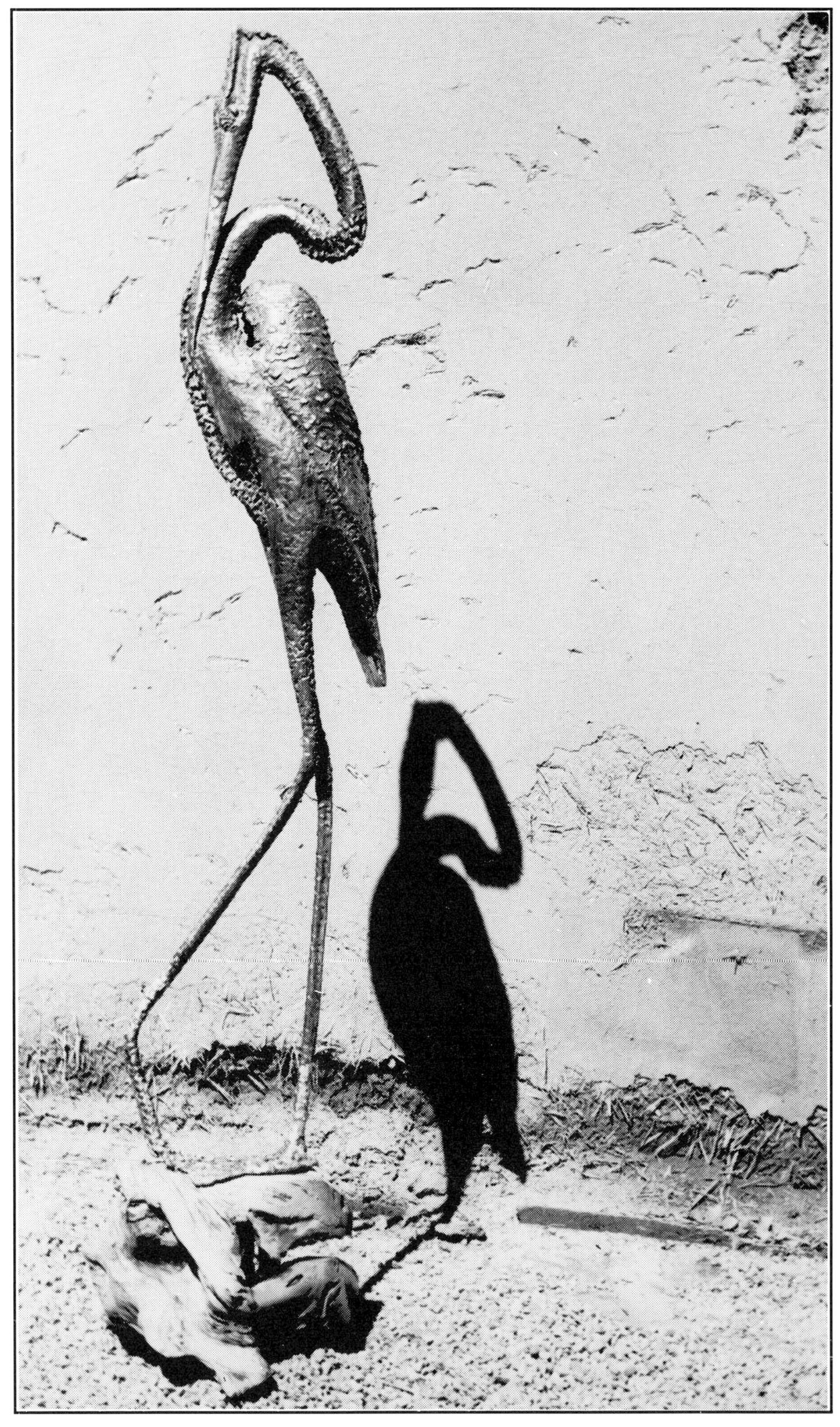

HERON, bronze (1963) 57''

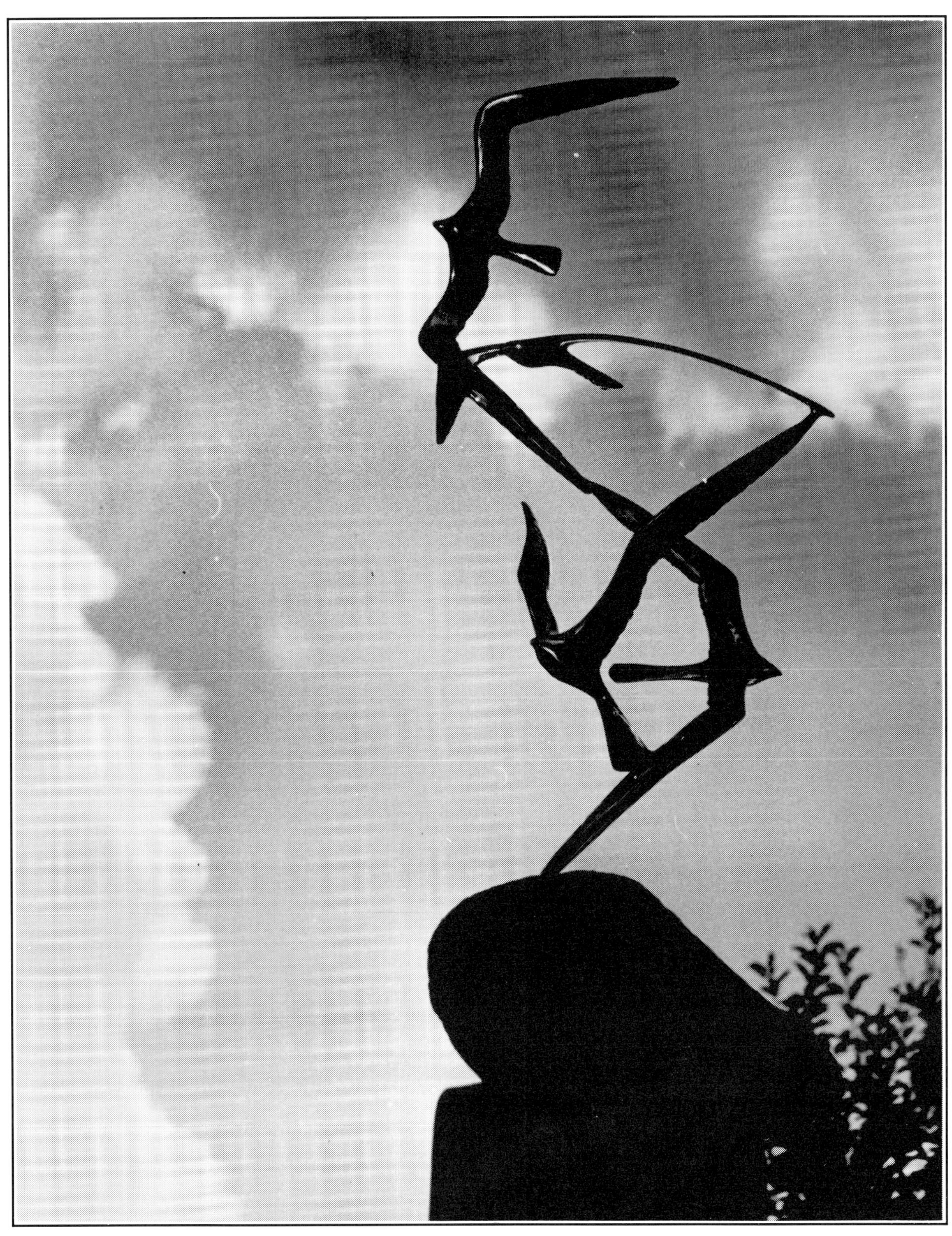

EVENING SILHOUETTE, bronze (1966) 58''

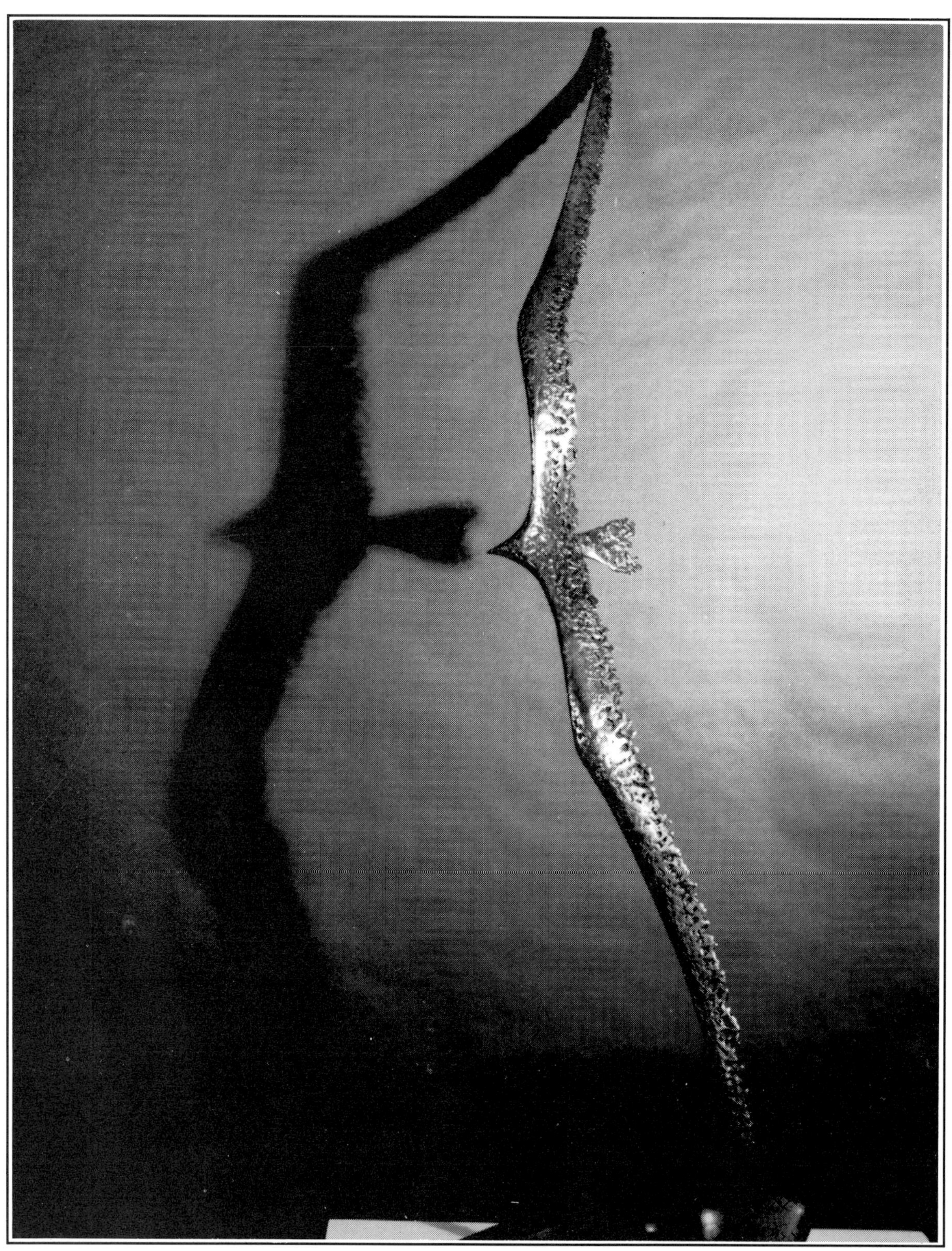

MORNING MIST, bronze, silver (1972) 96''

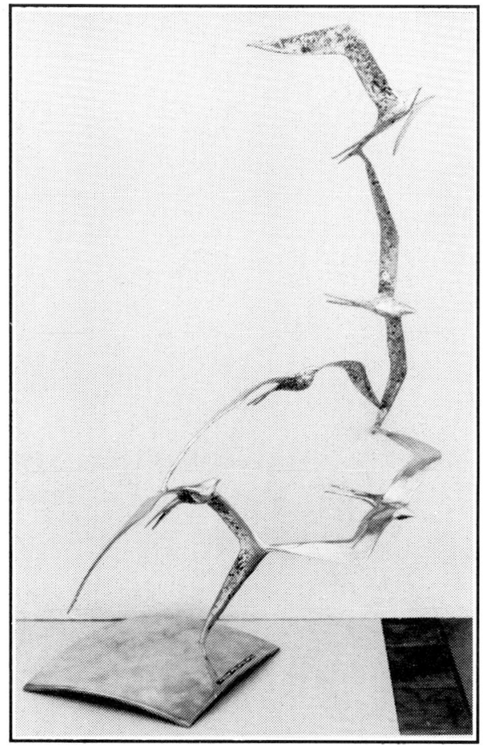

SEA BIRDS, bronze (1970) 48''

DUET, bronze (1968) 42''

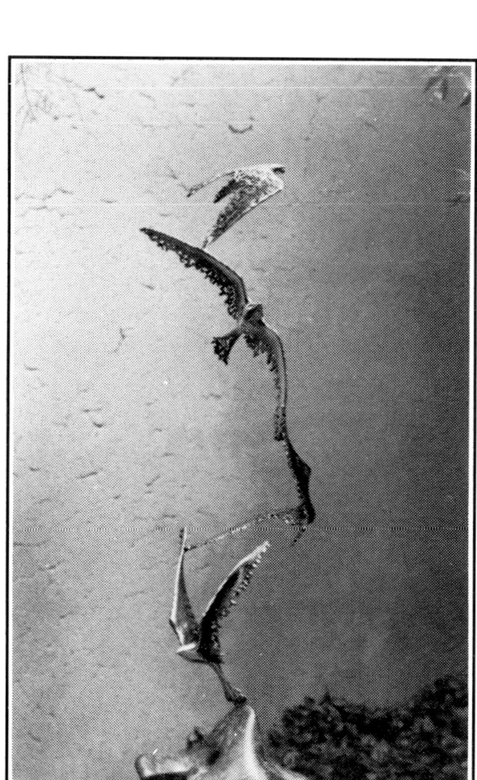

SOARING BIRDS, bronze (1970) 48''

ON THE WIND, Mobile, bronze (1967)
on tapered iron rod, 108''

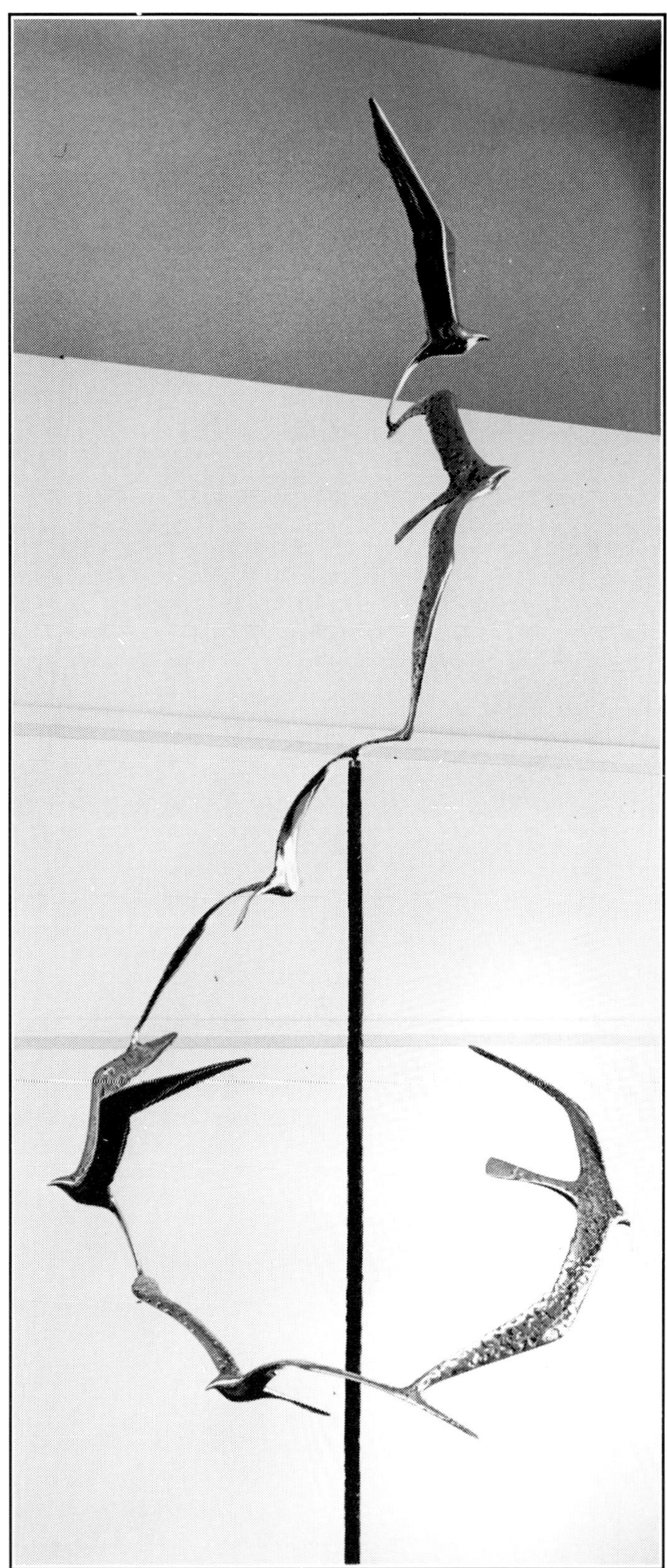

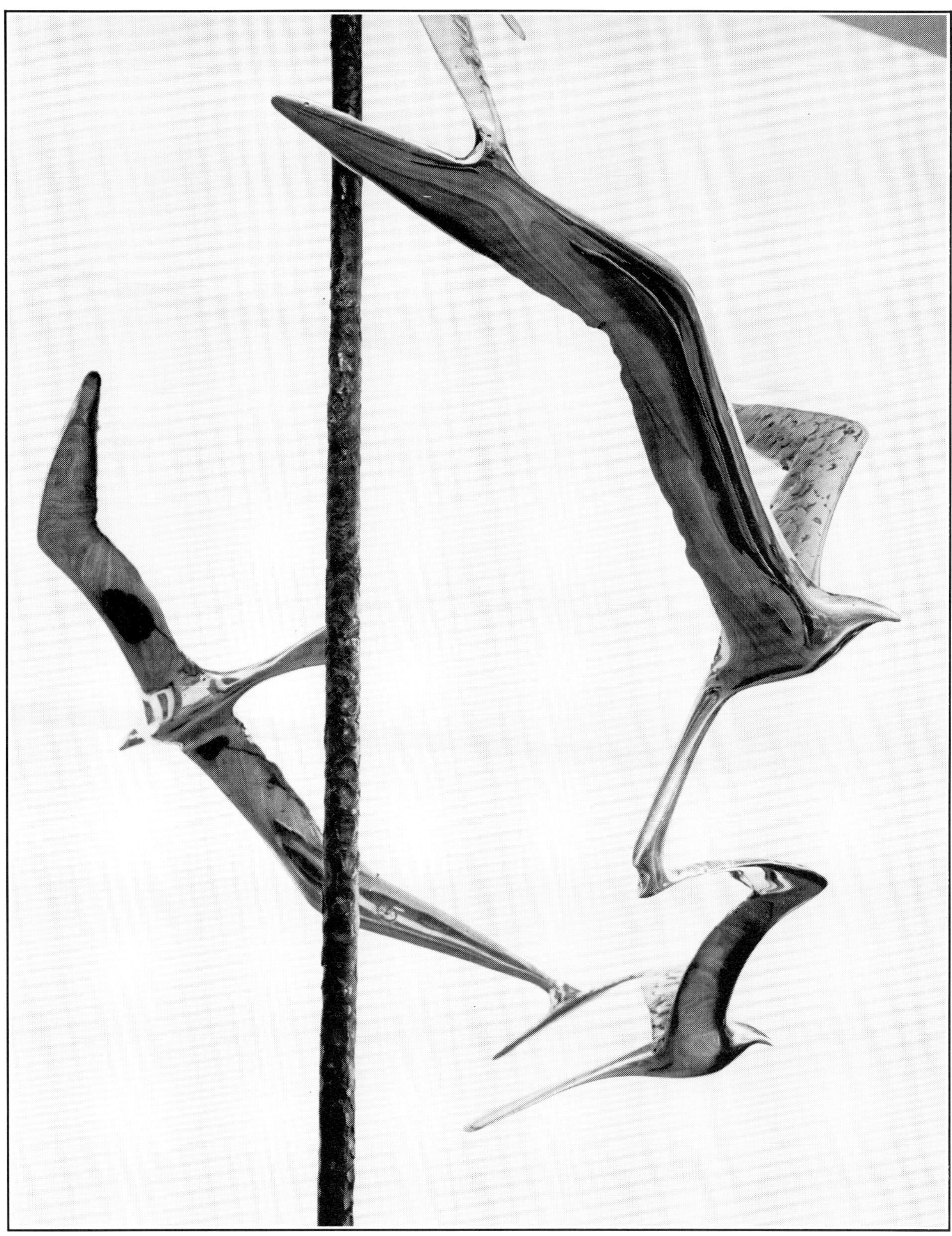

Detail of ON THE WIND

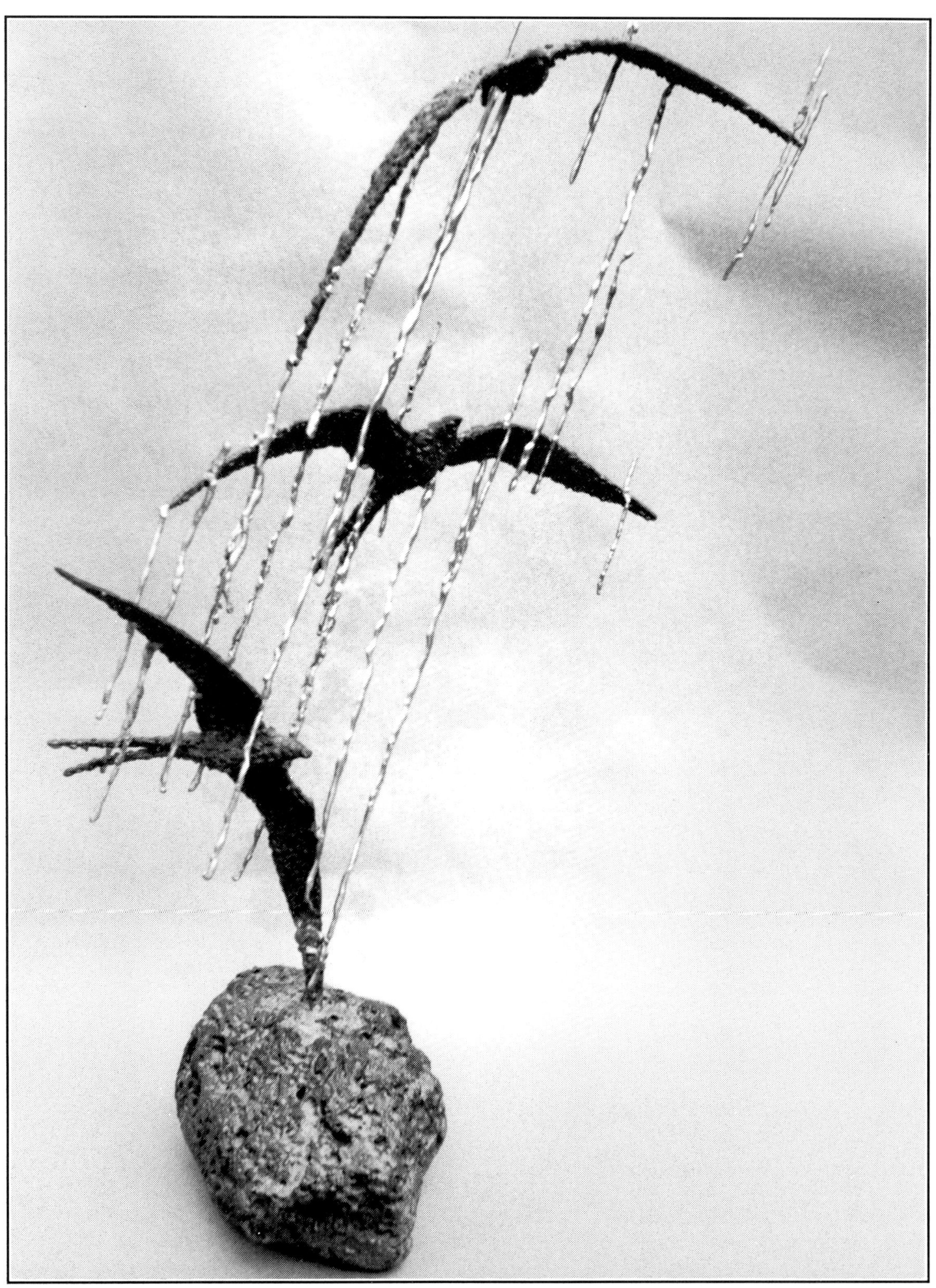

RAIN BIRDS, bronze (1972) 38'' x 22'' x 12'', wing span each bird 18''

HUMOR

Humor—often sophisticated, often satirical—infused much of Gilbertson's work. Animals typically served as the medium for the message.

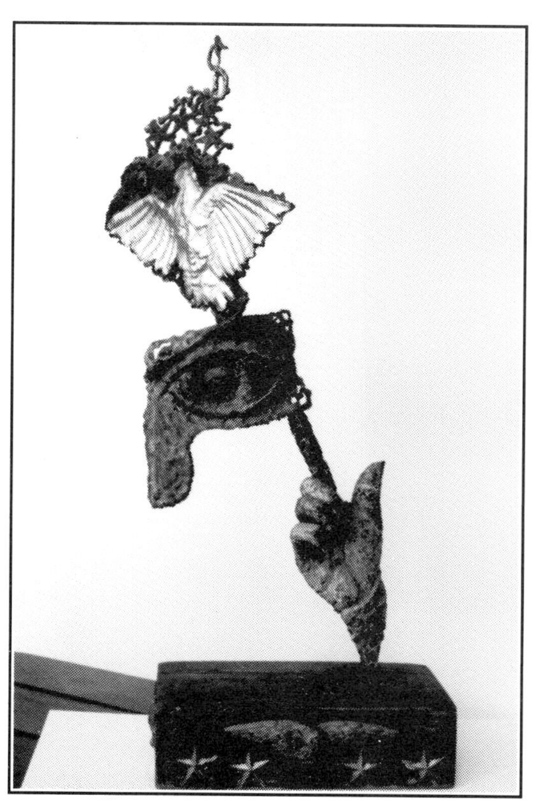

BIG BROTHER'S EYE IS ON YOU,
corten steel, gold leaf (1970) 27'' x 11''

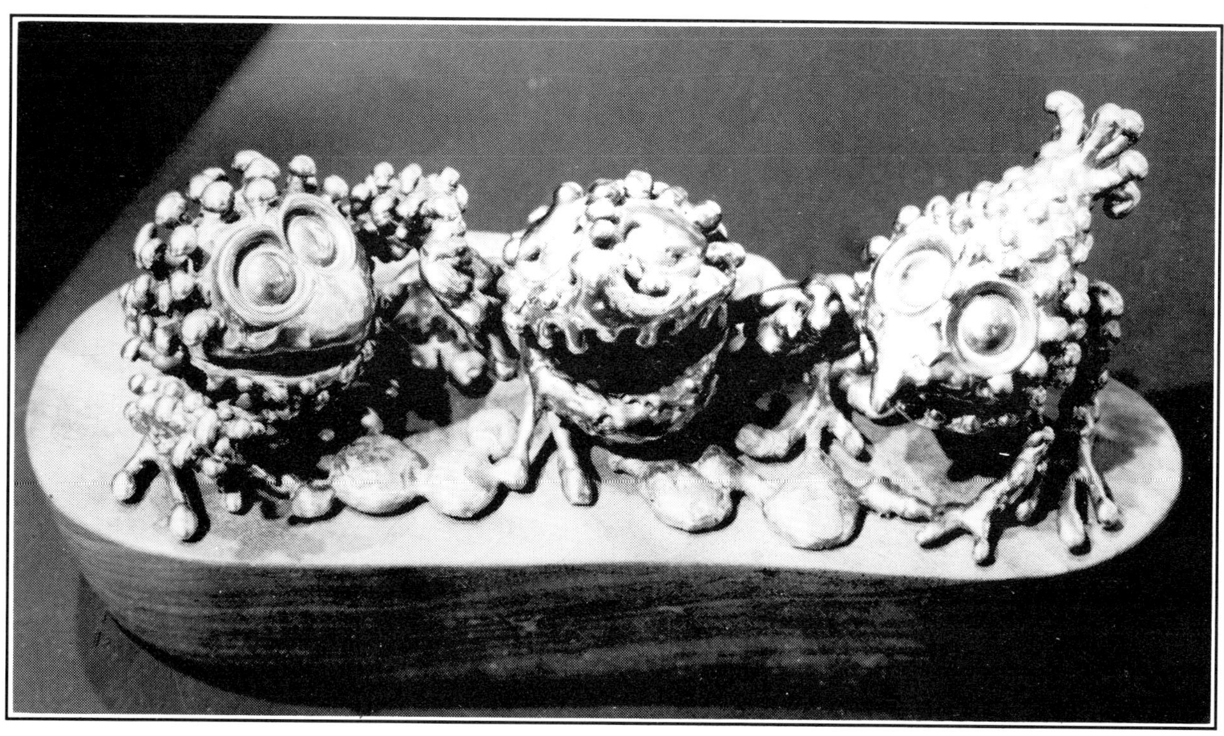

POLITICIANS, copper washed bronze (1970) 4'' x 8''

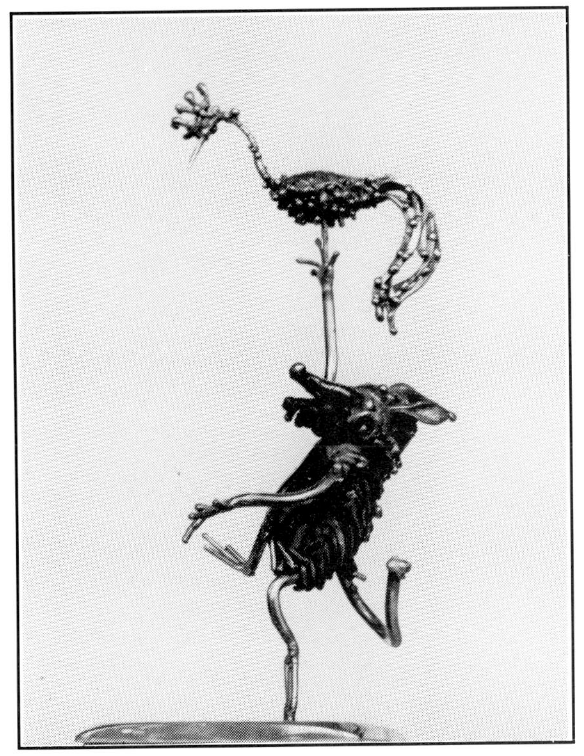

FOR THE PSYCHIATRIST
WHO HAS EVERYTHING,
bronze (1965) 13''

MEANWHILE, BACK AT THE
PENTAGON,
bronze (1968) 12''

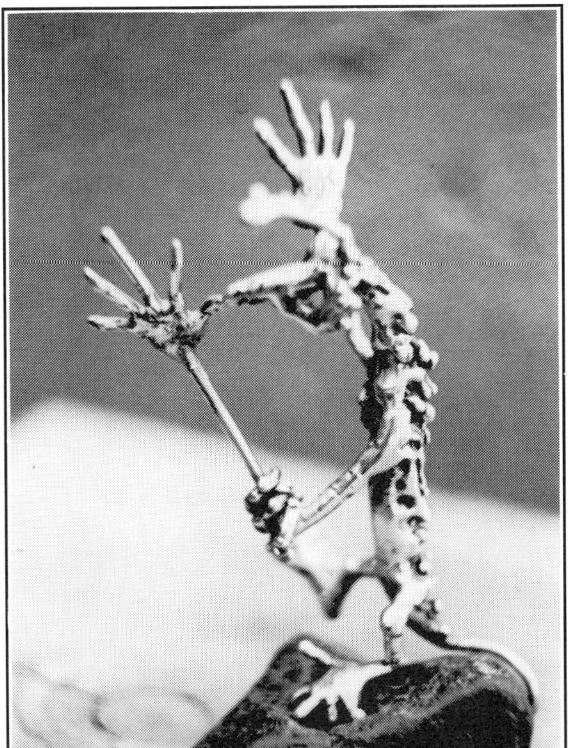

WHAT THE HELL,
bronze (1963) 6''

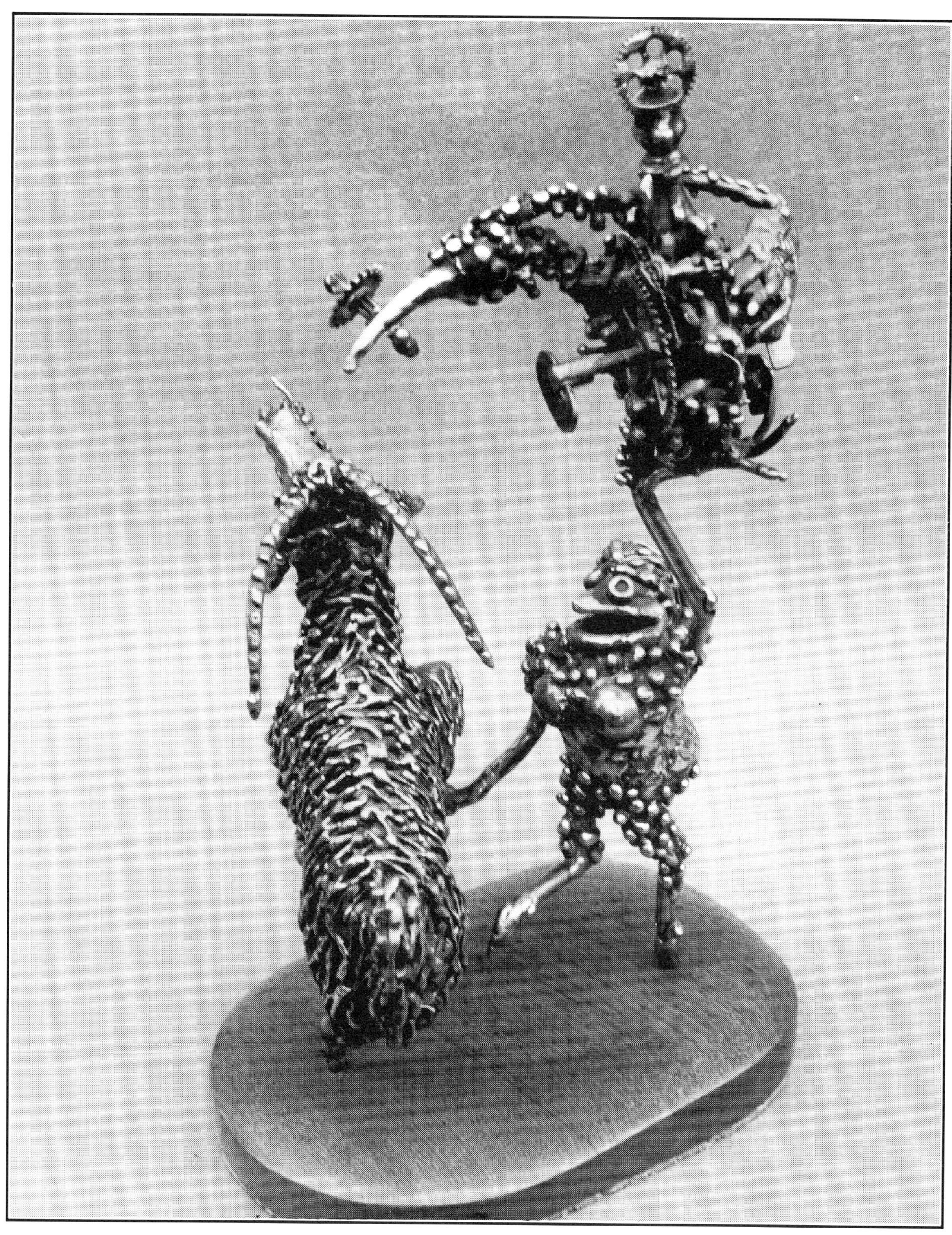

CYBERNETIC WALTZ, bronze (1968) 14'', 6'' x 7'' at base

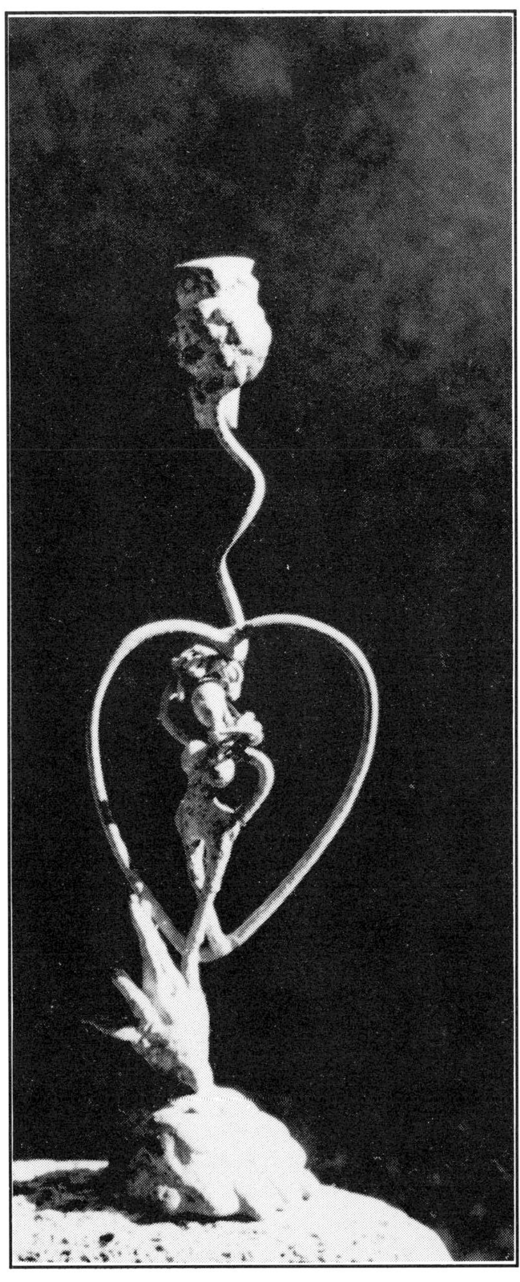

VALENTINE, patina bronze (c 1960) 10''

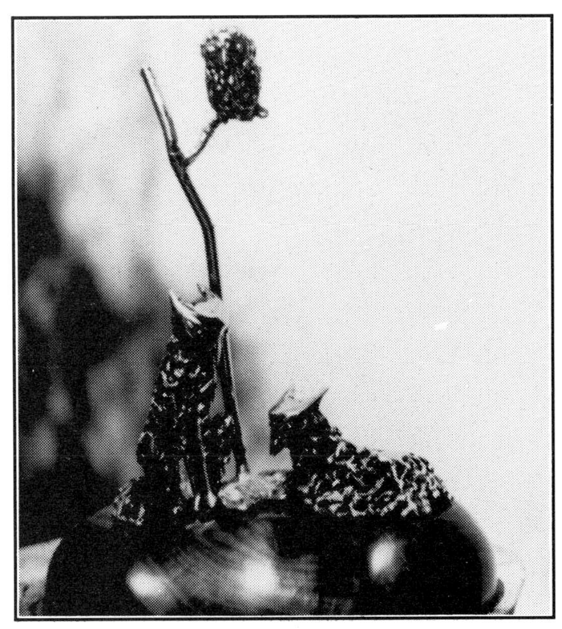

PATIENCE, bronze (1966) 6'' x 5''

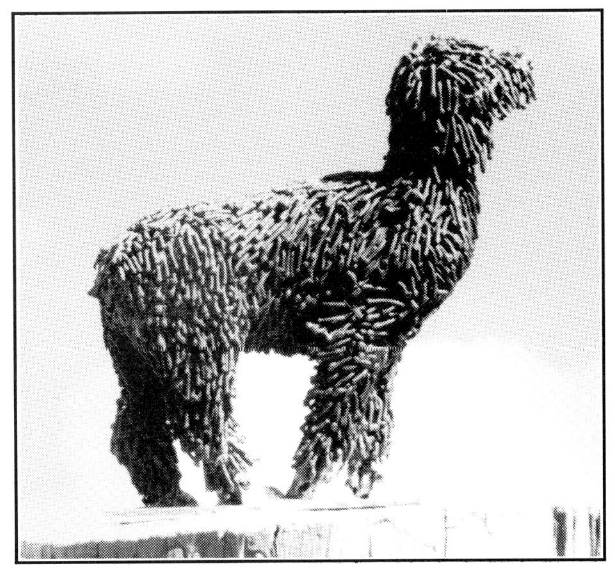

SHAGGY DOG, bronze (1962) 8'' x 7''

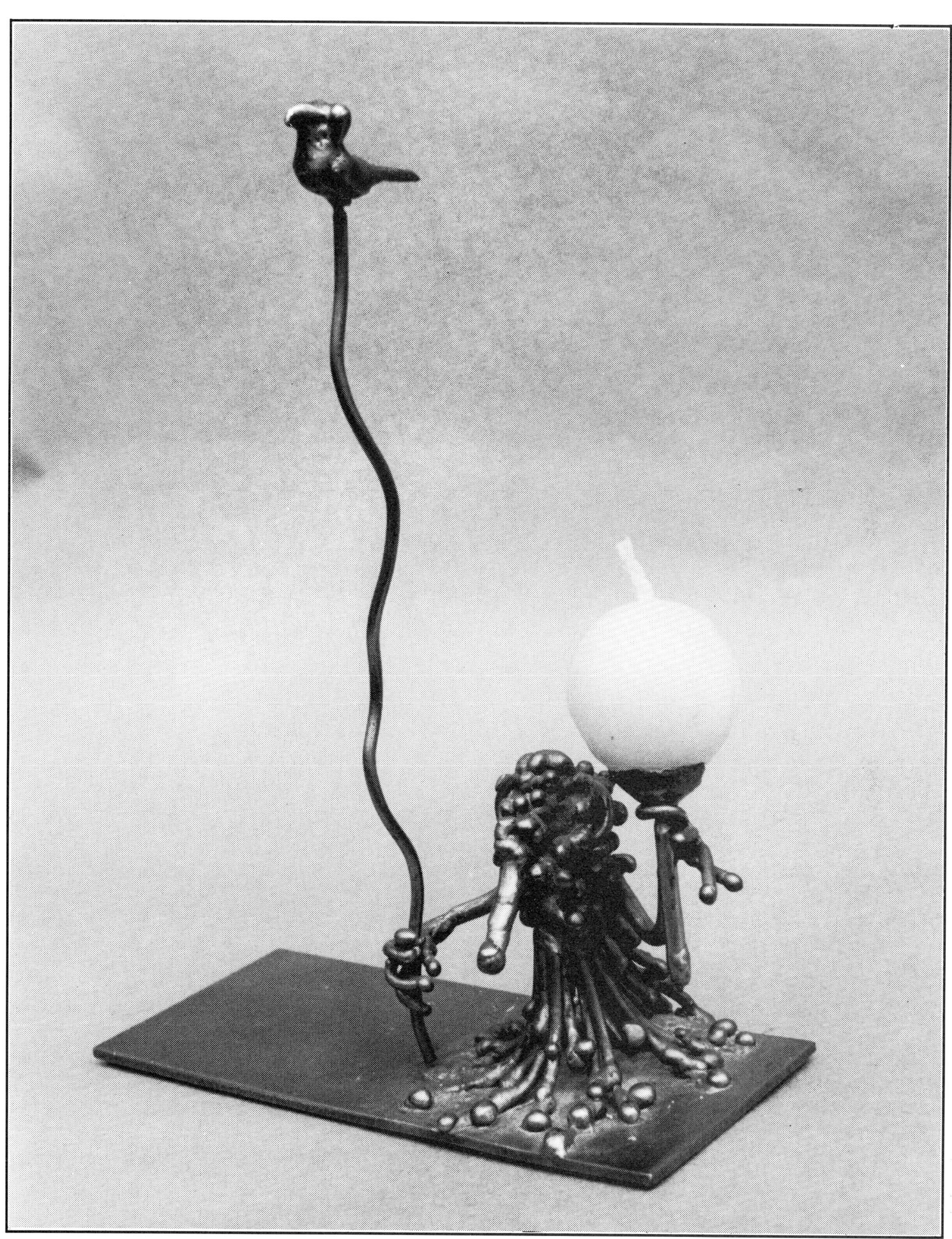

UPWARD AND ONWARD, bronze (1965) 9'', base 3'' x 7''

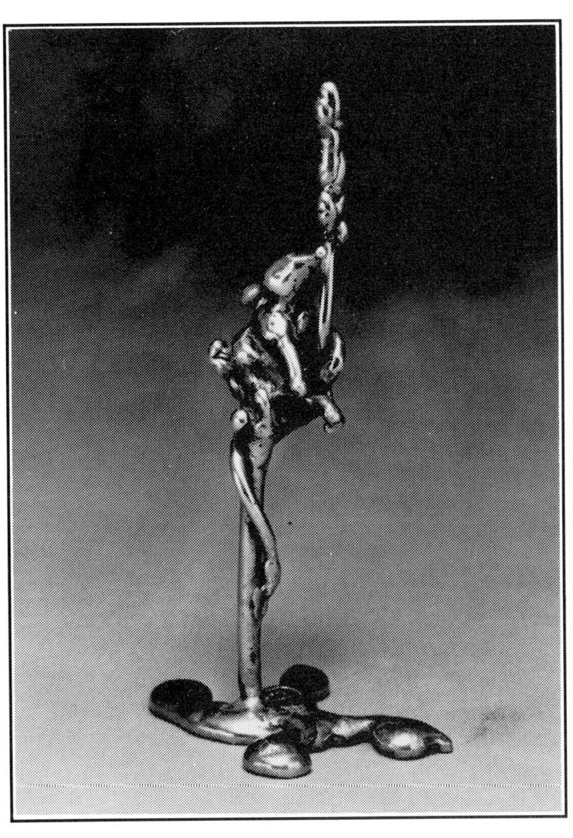

MOUSE, bronze (1964) 5″

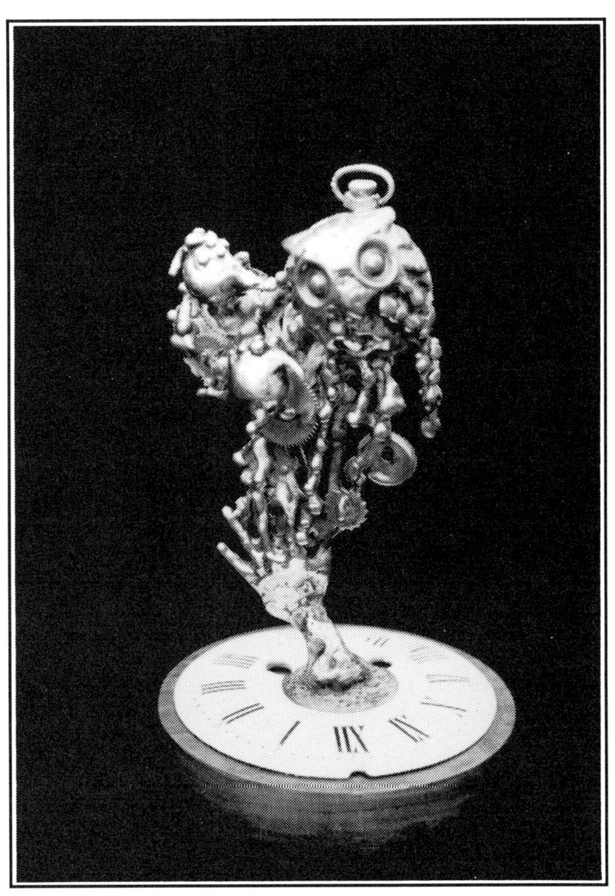

TIME IS FOR THE BIRDS, bronze (1975) 10″

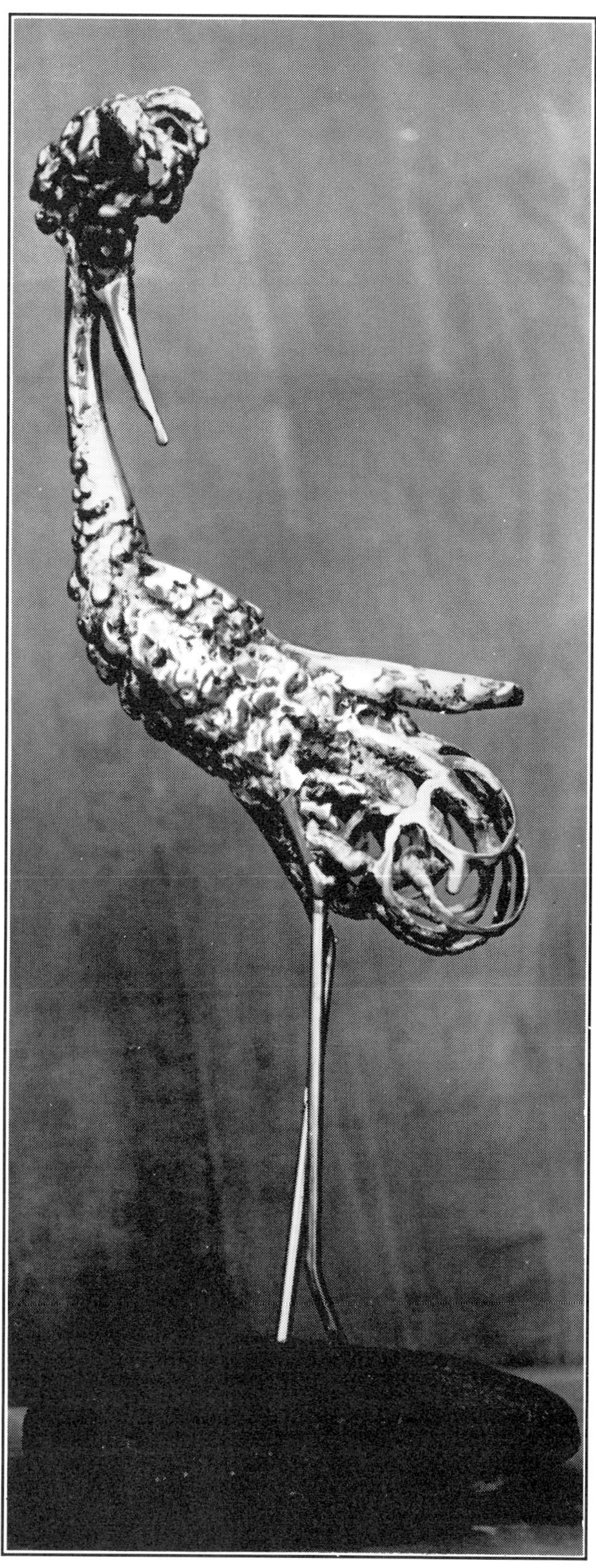

COQUETTE, bronze (1970) 12''

JEWELRY

Gilbertson made jewelry for the sheer pleasure of creating it, never commercially, only for close friends. Most of the pieces were repoussé, the pendants interchangeable on a choker of twisted gold and silver wire.

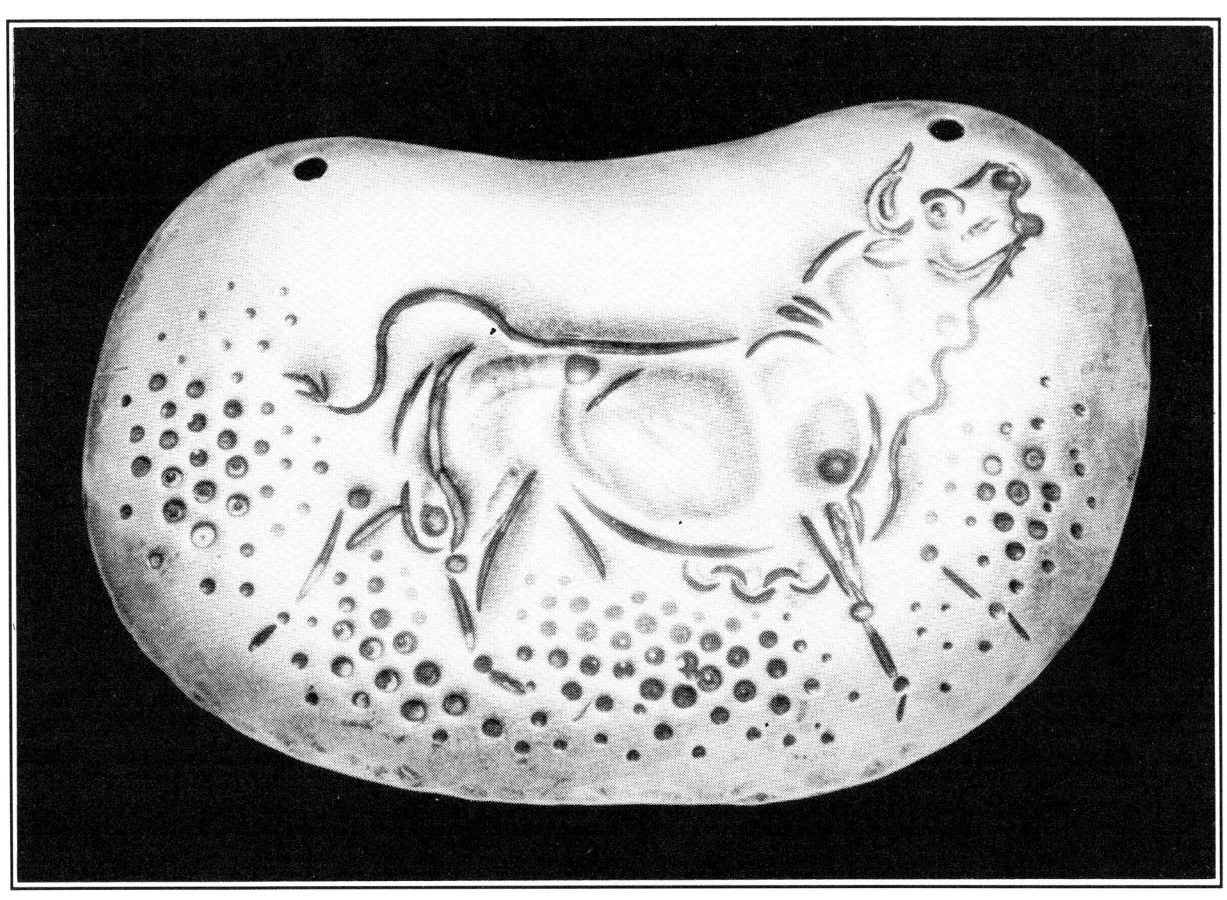

BULL PENDANT, silver repoussé (1953) 3″ x 4½″   Photo: Stephen Piersol

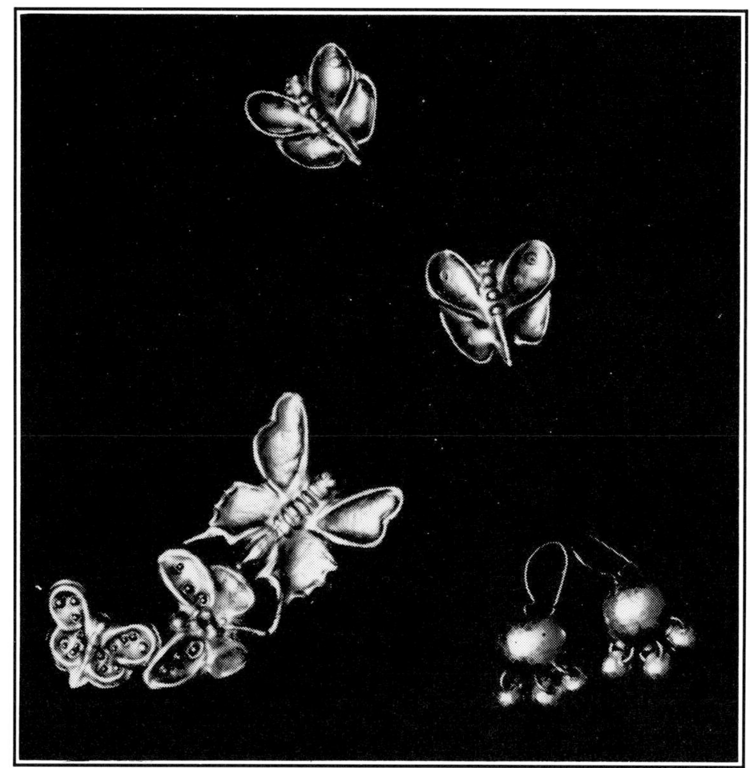

BUTTERFLY EARRINGS,
gold 1''

BUTTERFLY PENDANT,
silver, gold 3½''

DANGLE EARRINGS, gold ¾''

(all 1975)

Photo: Stephen Piersol

DOVE PIN, silver (1944) 2'' x ¾''

HEART PENDANT,
silver (1955) 2½''

OWL PENDANT,
silver, gold (1970) 3½''

MONKEY PENDANT, carved
slate on silver (1945) 3½''

Photo: Stephen Piersol

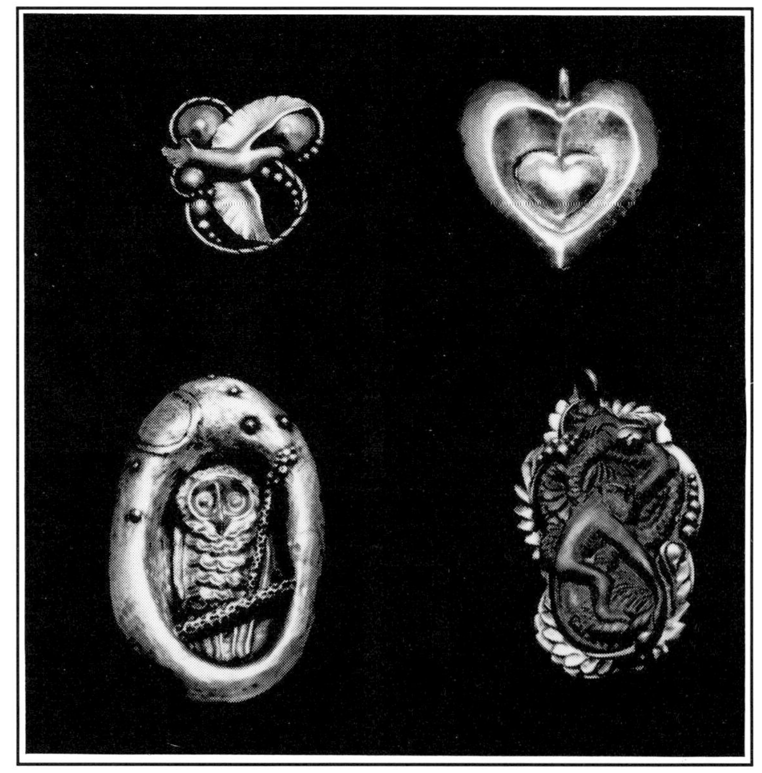

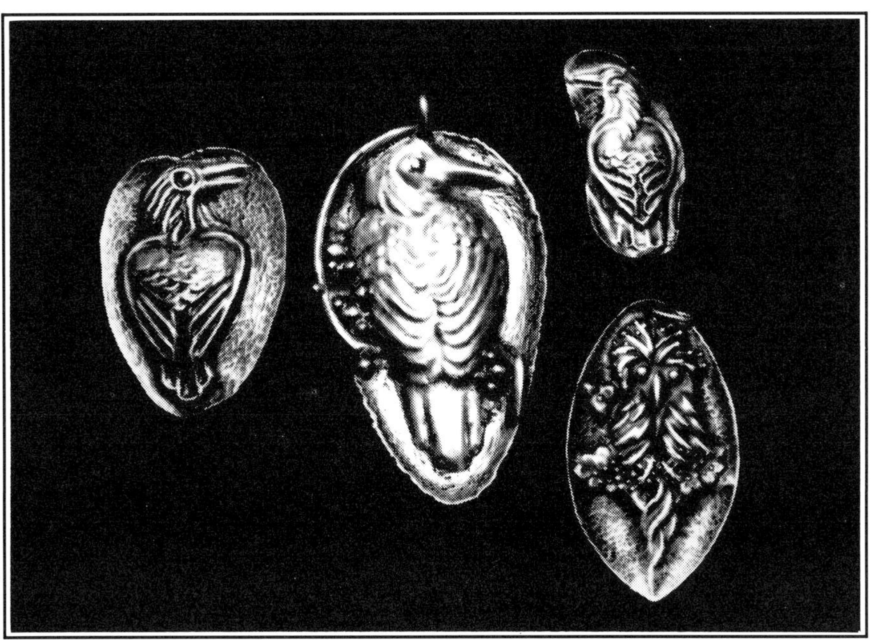

RAVEN PENDANTS, silver (c1970) 3'', 4½'', 2½'', 3¼''
Photo: Stephen Piersol

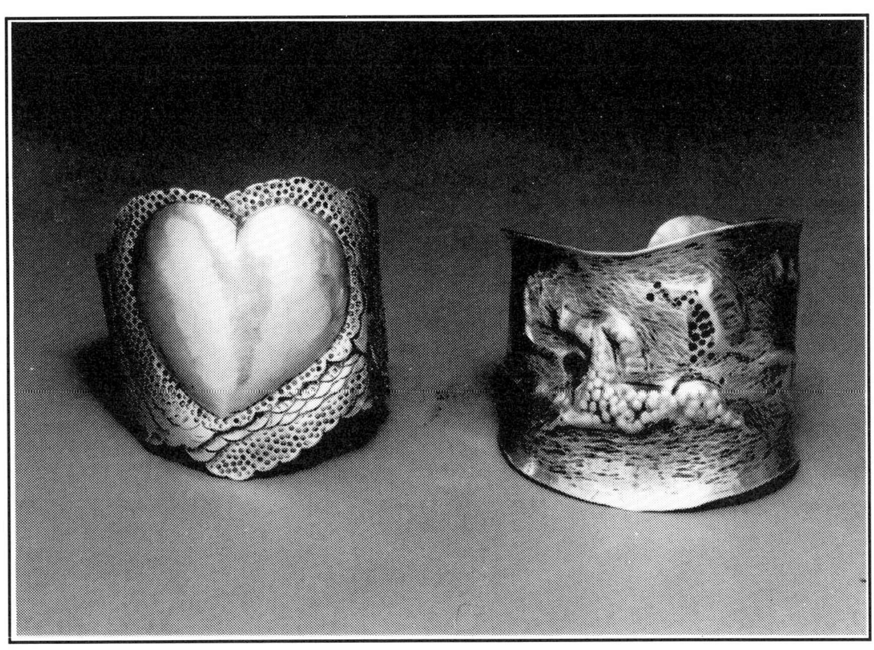

HEART BRACELET, silver (1940) width 2½''
BRACELET WITH HORSES, silver (1950) width 2½''
Photo: Stephen Piersol

CAT PENDANT, carved slate (1950) 4″

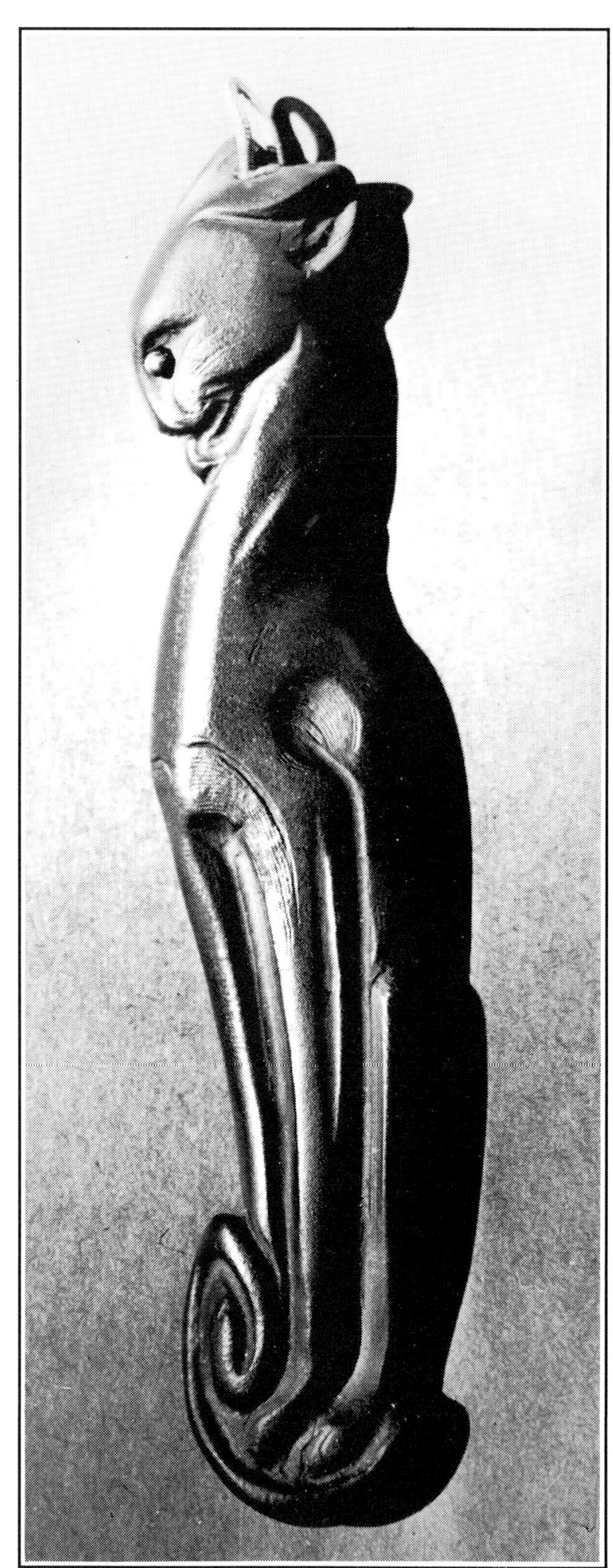

CHINESE BRUSH DRAWINGS

Gilbertson studied calligraphy in Chicago with Sensai Ogura. He found it relaxing to get out his precious bamboo brushes of all sizes with whiskers of various animals, to sit quietly grinding sticks or pieces of old fragrant inks on slabs of satin-smooth slate, using only beautiful handmade Japanese papers.

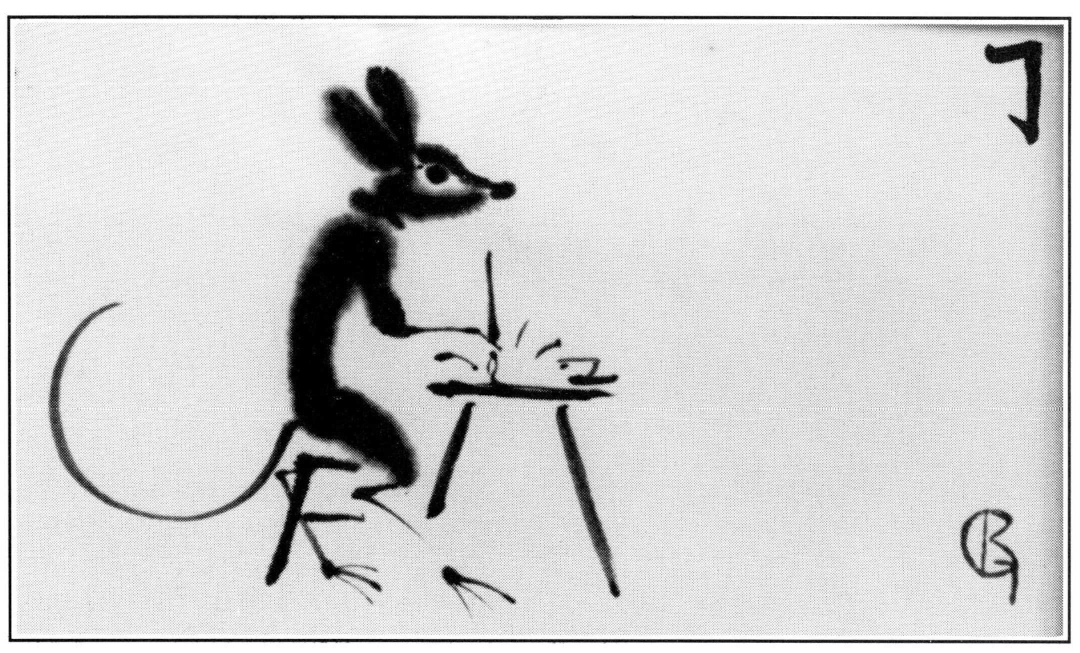

SELF PORTRAIT (1960) 7'' x 12½''
All Photos: Erwin Jakobs

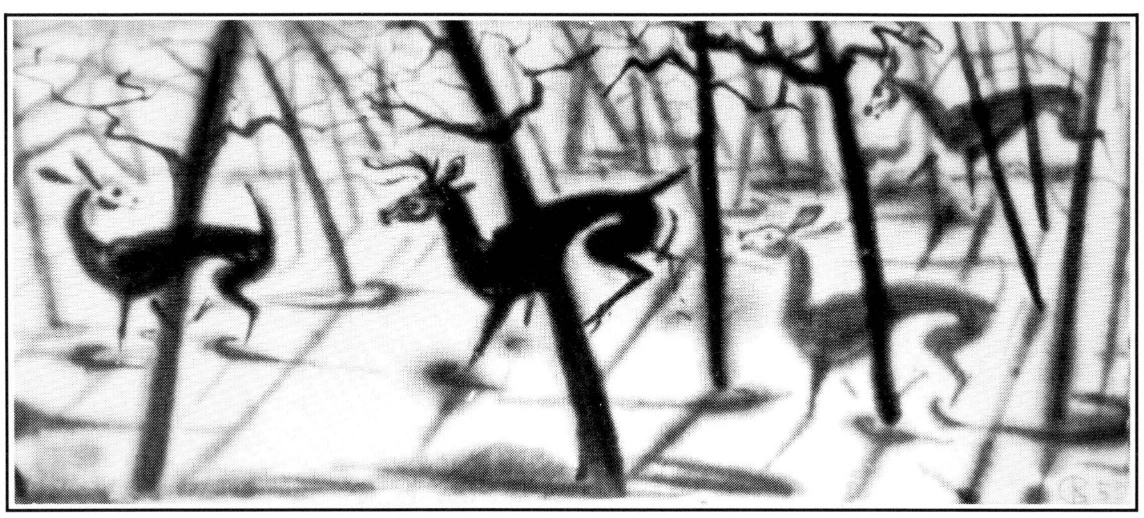

RUNNING DEER (1959) 9'' x 21''

TORERO (1958) 18'' x 12½''

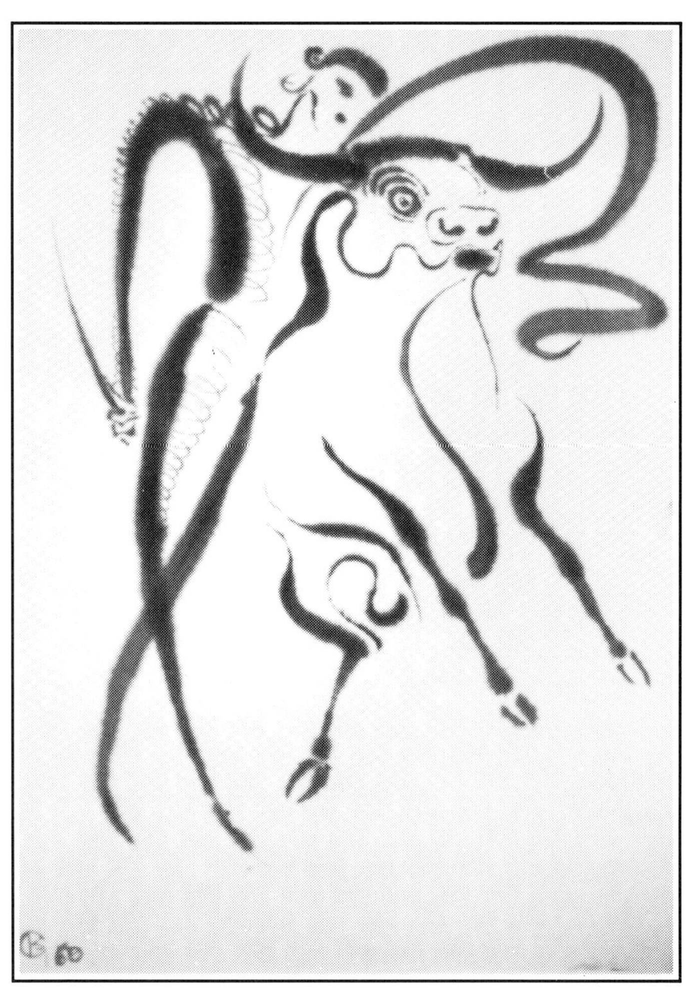

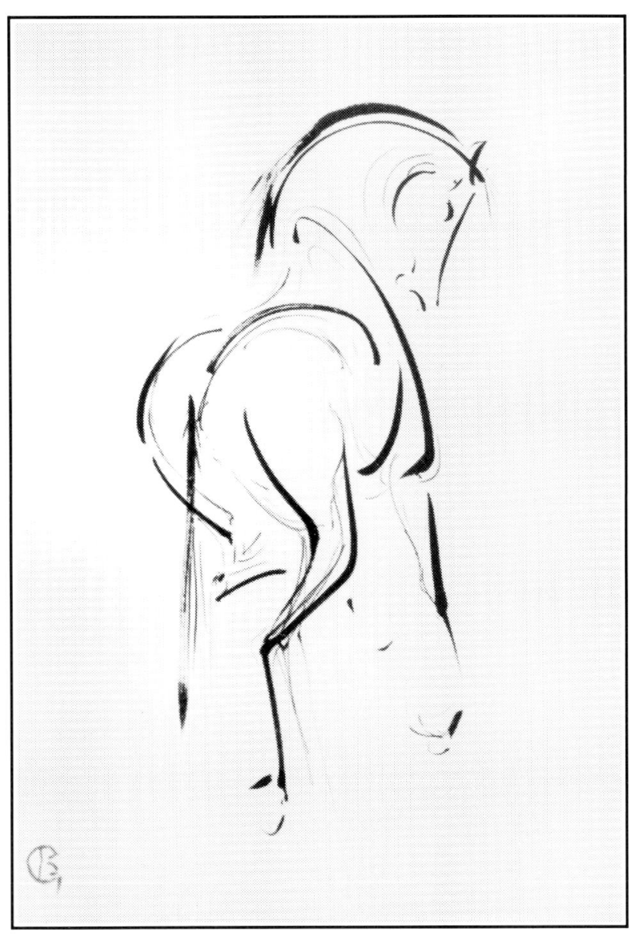

HORSE #5 (1952) 12½'' x 8''

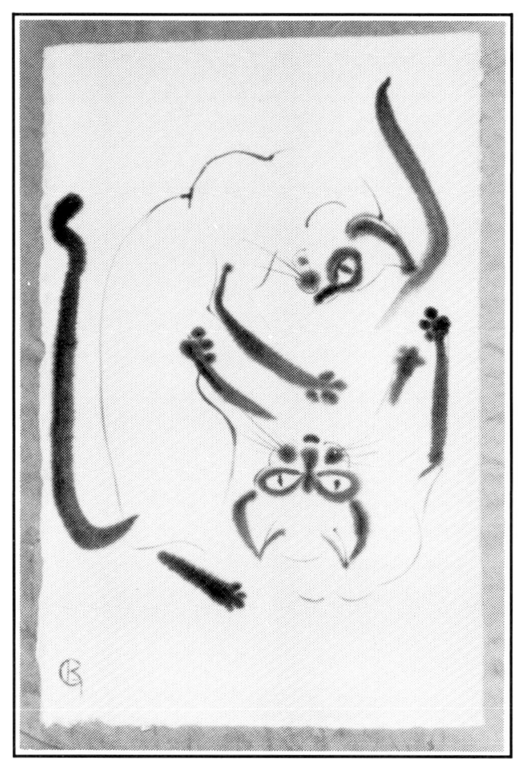

PLAYING CATS (1959) 12½'' x 12''

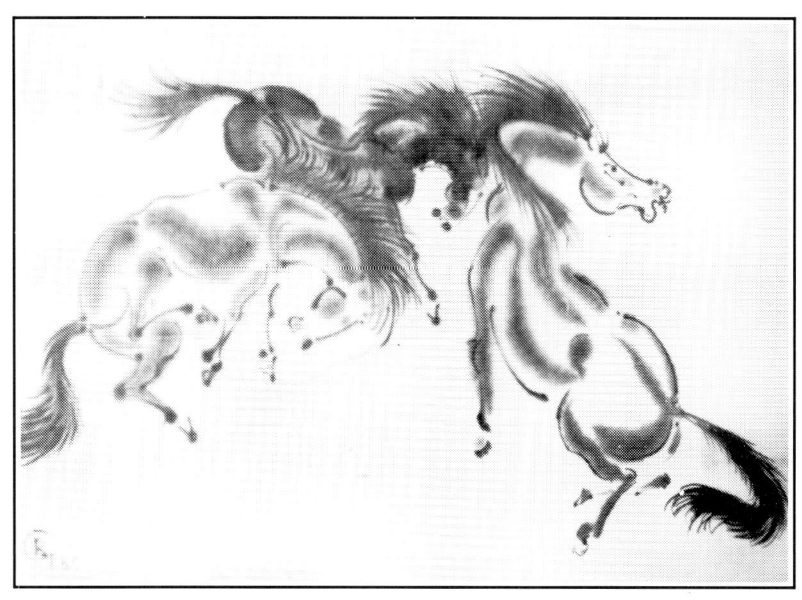

MUSTANGS (1958)
15½'' x 22''

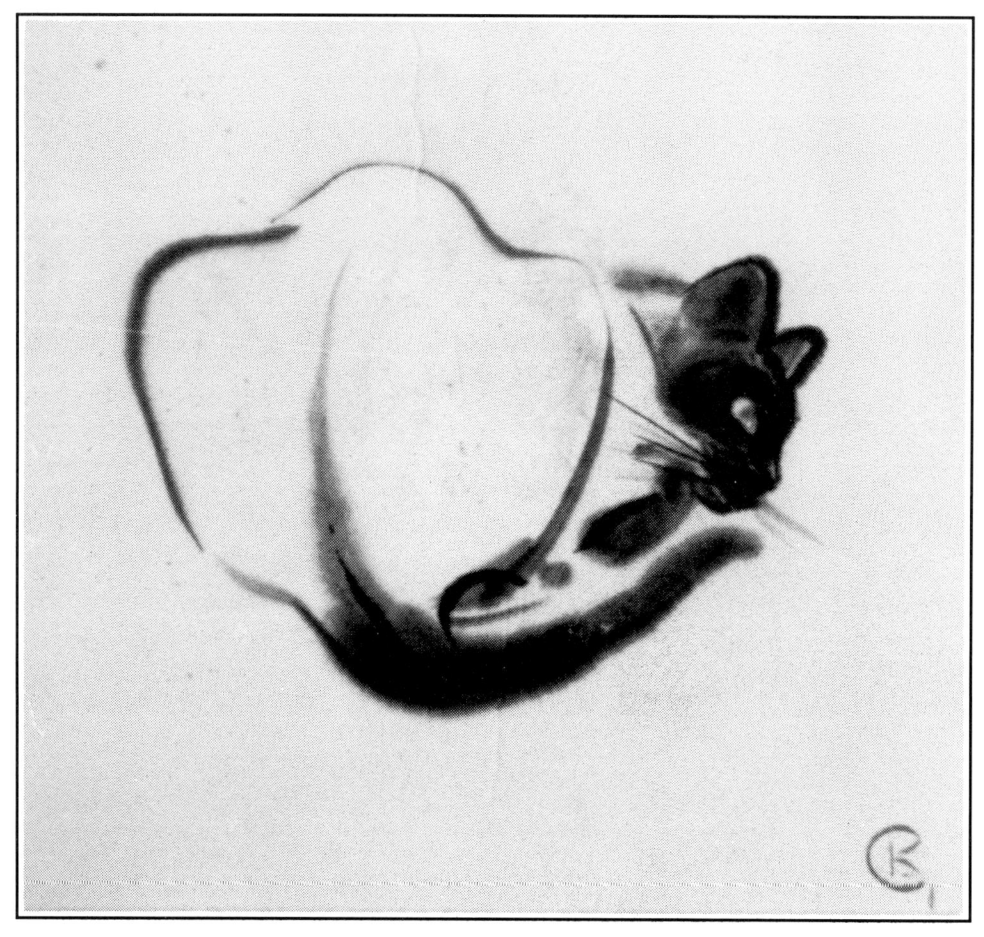

SIAMESE CAT (1959) 12'' x 12½''

THREE CATS (1956) 19'' x 12½''

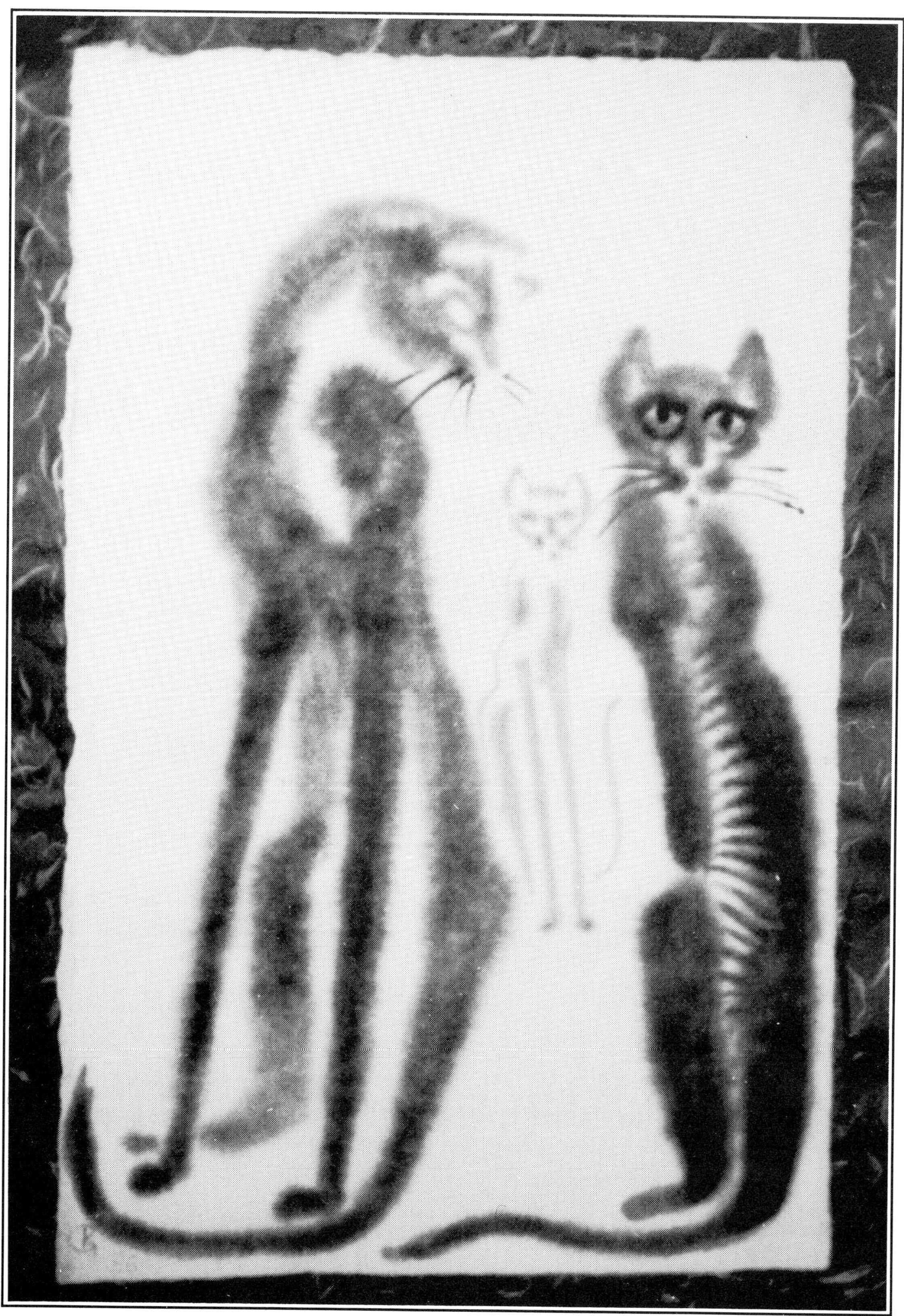

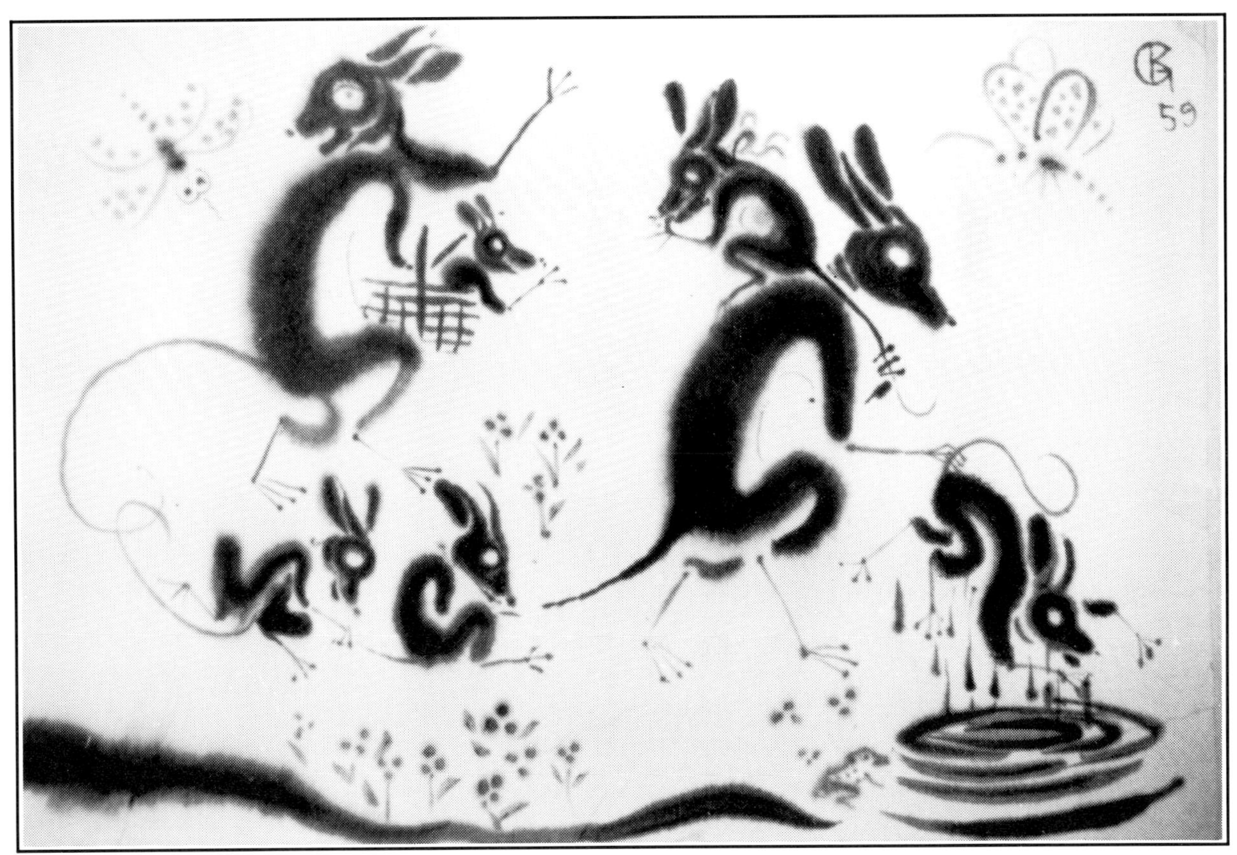

PICNIC (1959) 12'' x 18½''

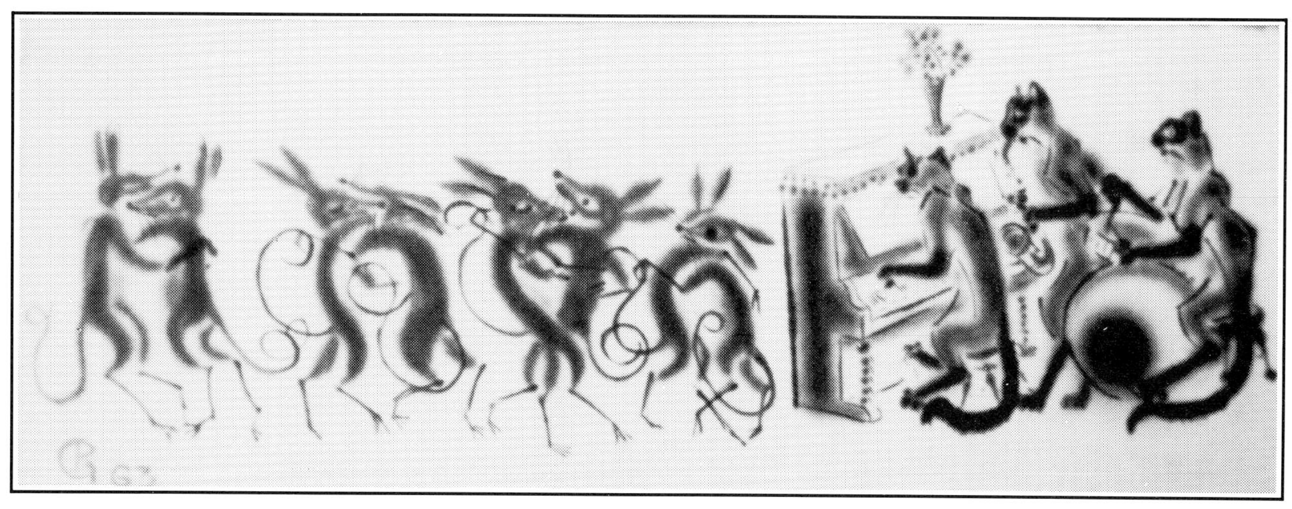

SATURDAY NIGHT SPECIAL (1958) 8½'' x 23''

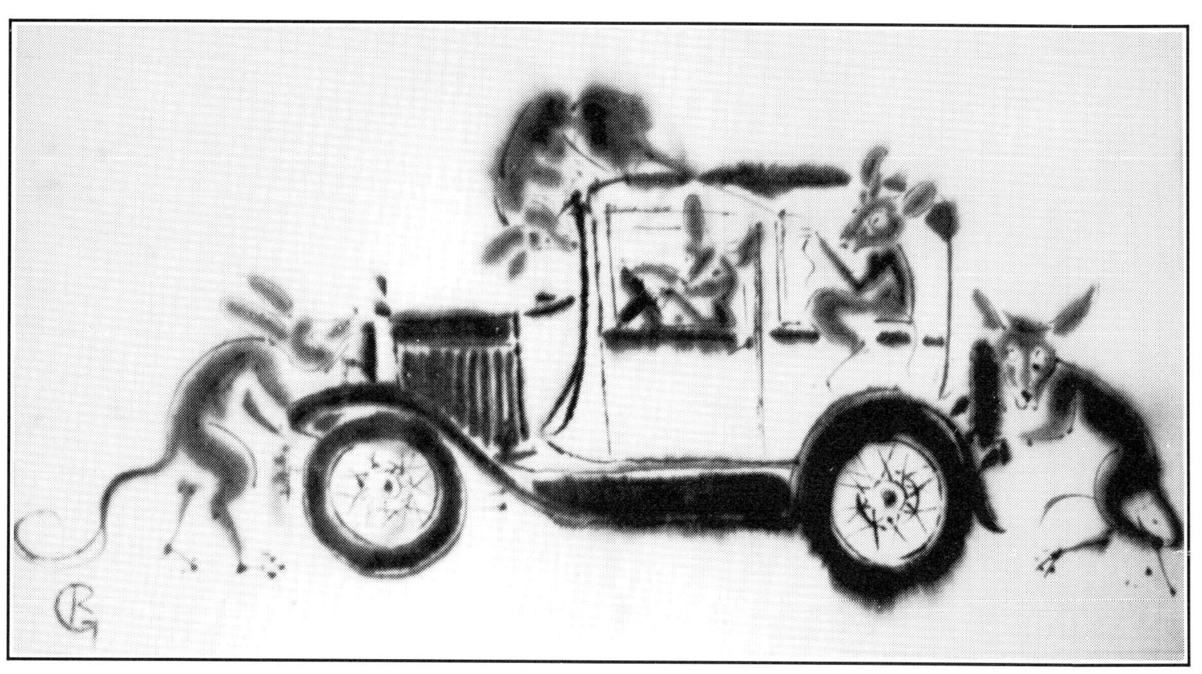

TROUBLES (1959) 8½'' x 23''

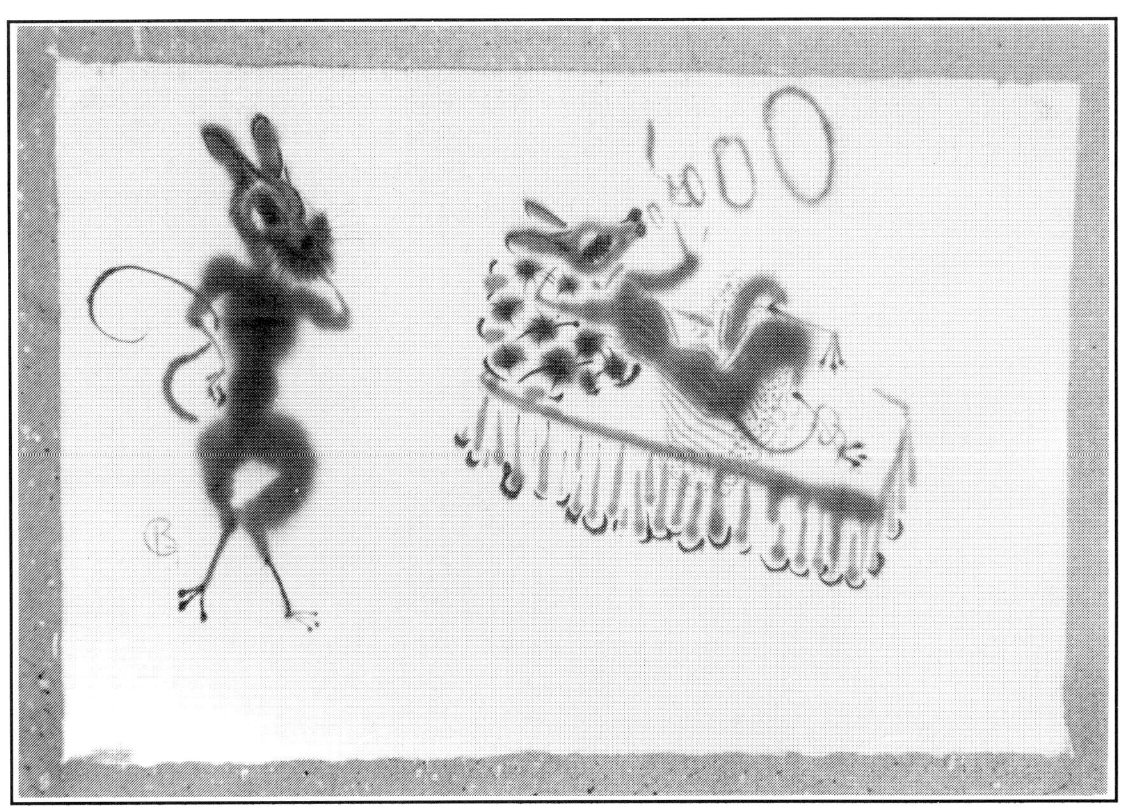

SPRING THOUGHTS
(1962) 12½'' x 18''

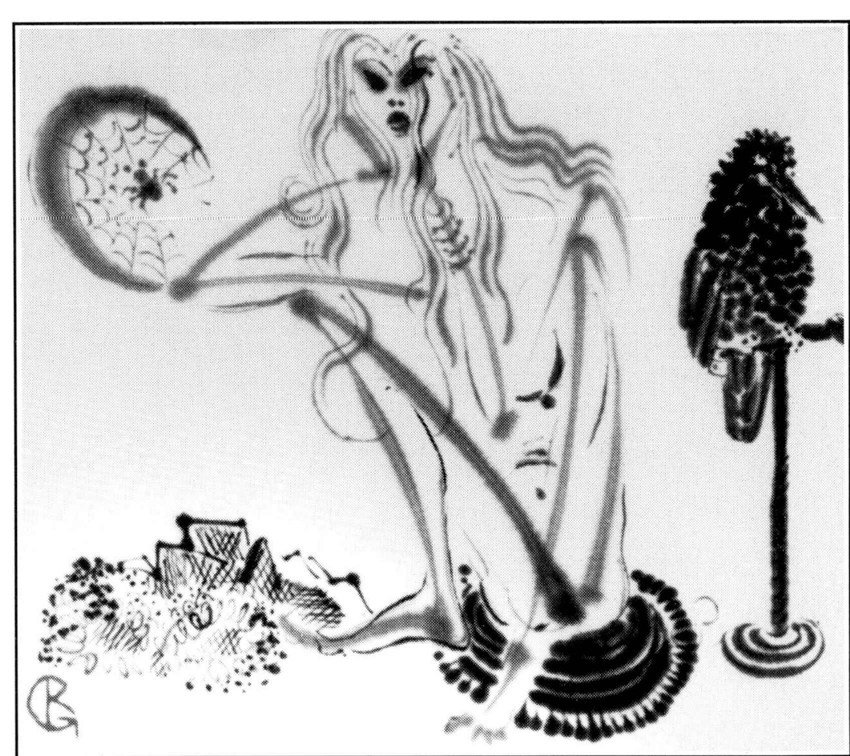

LA BRUJA (1958)
9½'' x 11''

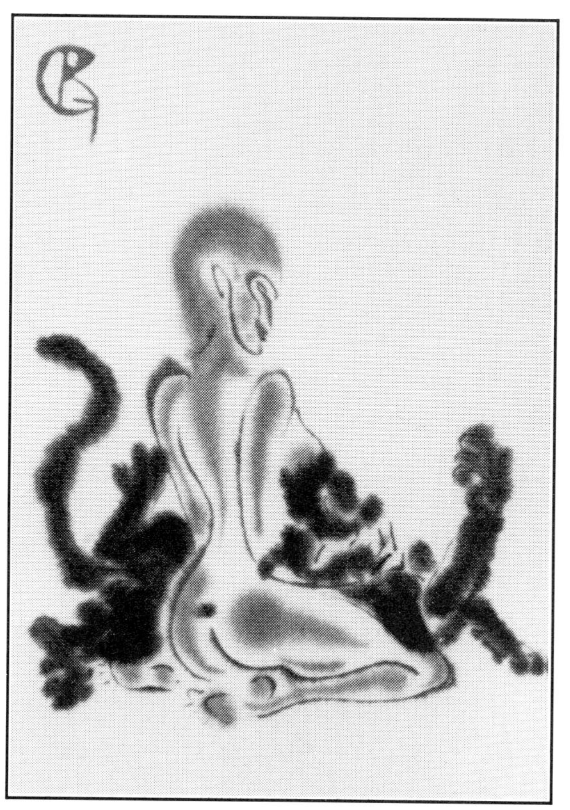

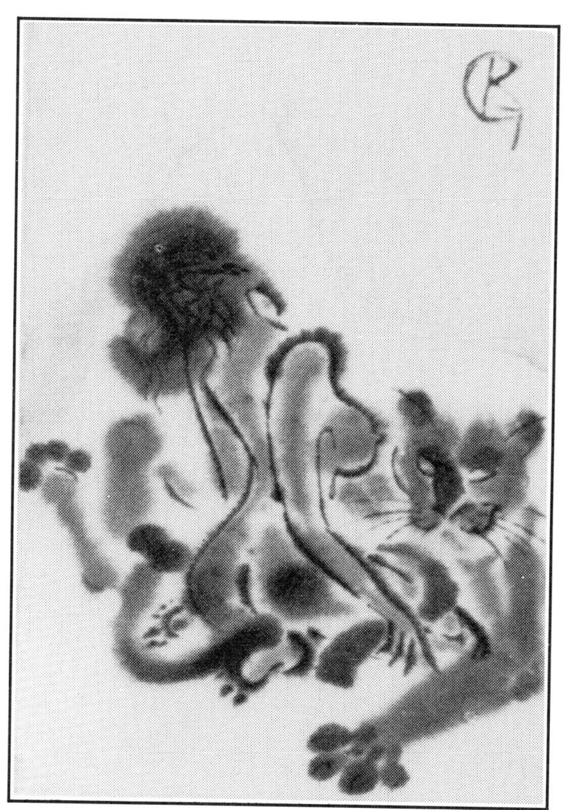

LEDA 6'' x 8''

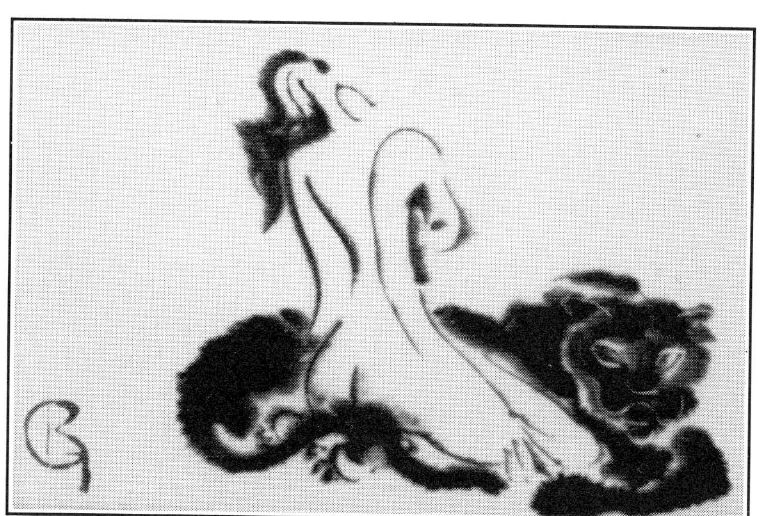

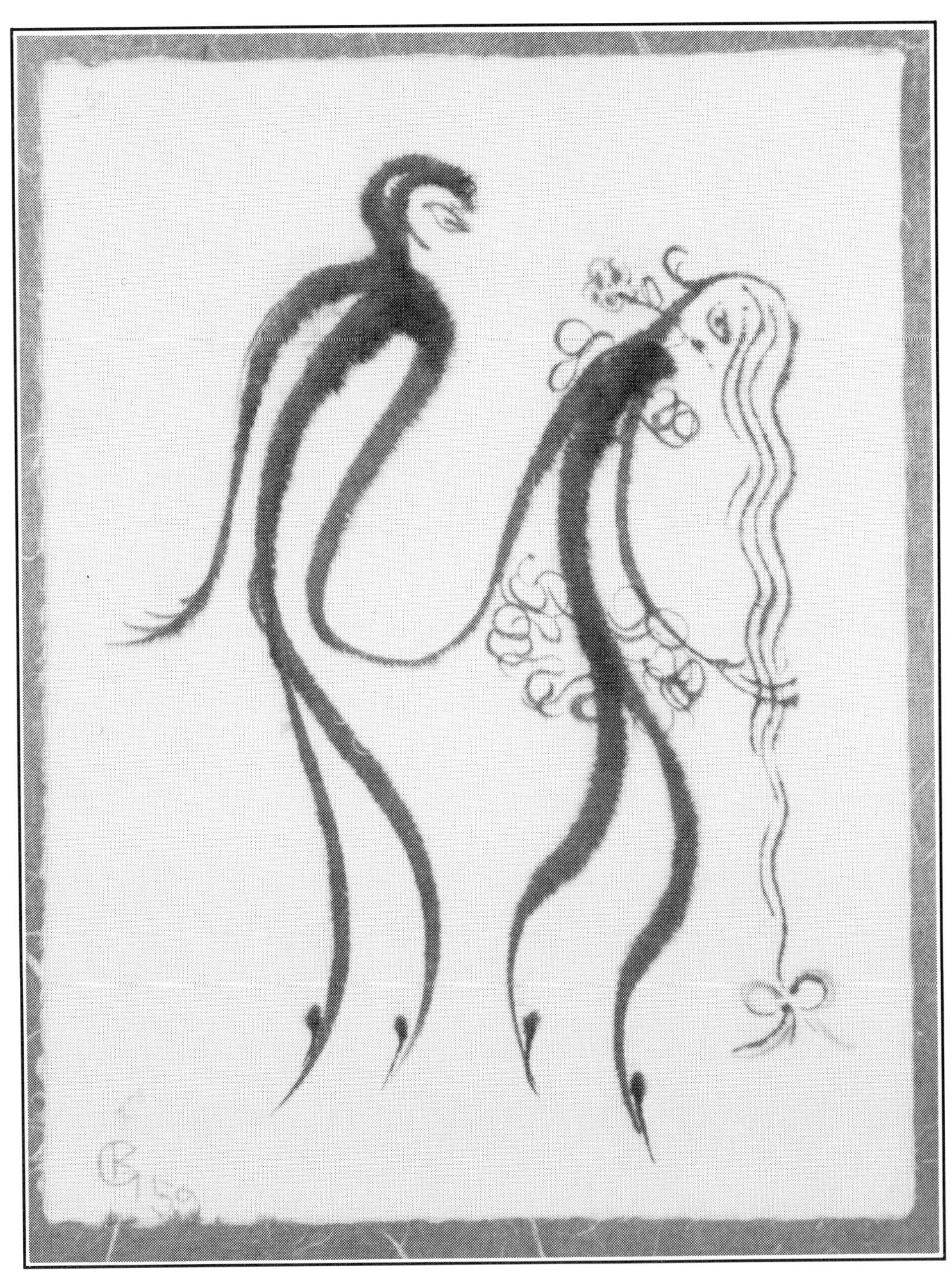

PAS DE DEUX (1964) 16'' x 12''

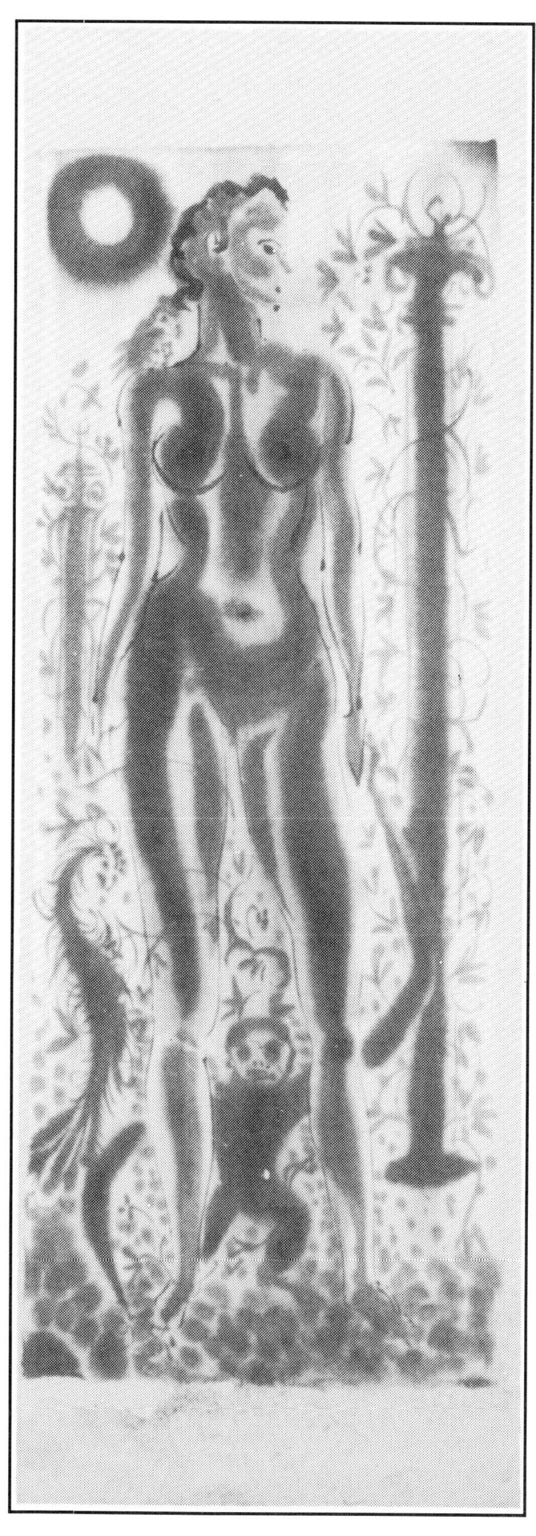

NUDE AND PARROT (1954) 25'' x 9½''

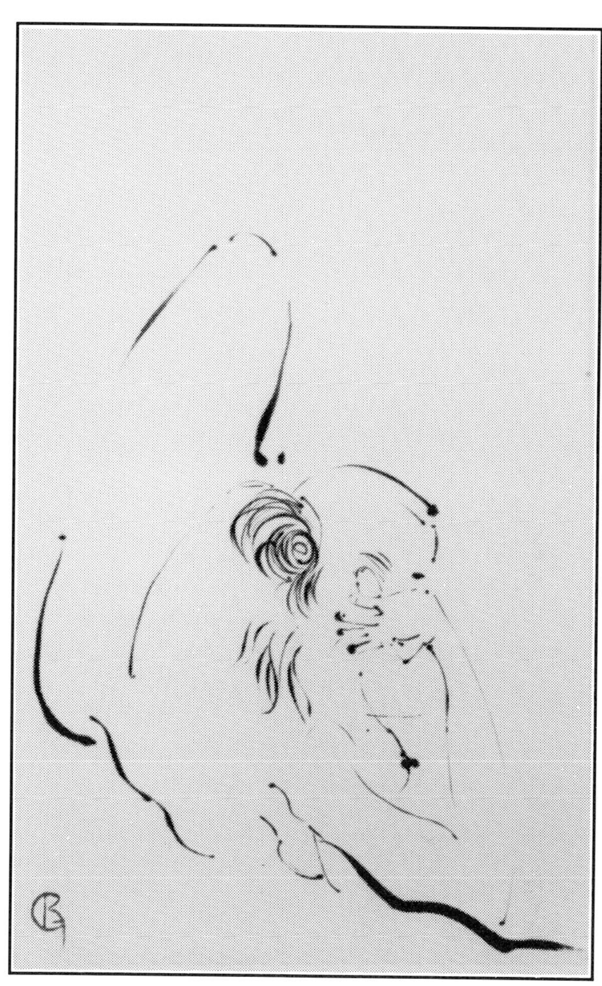

NUDE SKETCH (1954) 18½'' x 12''

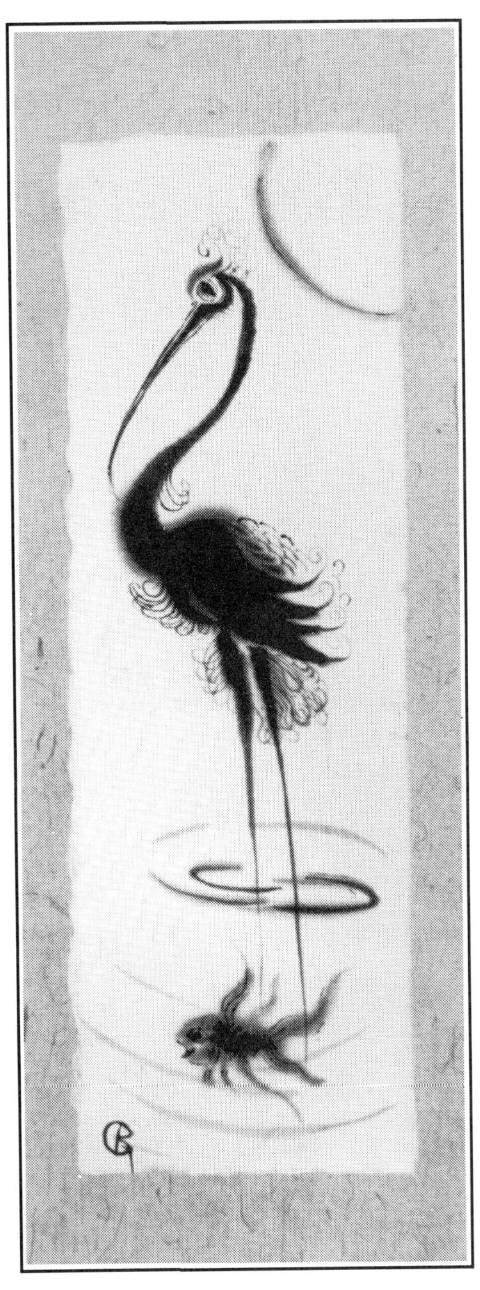

WADING HERON (1952) 18'' x 6''

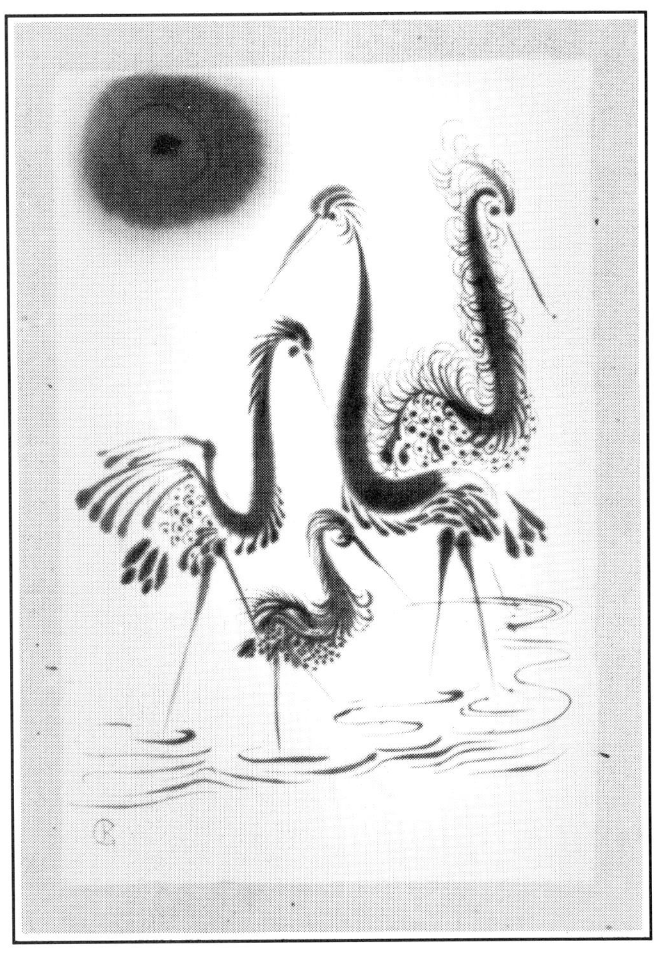

FOUR SILLY BIRDS (1959) 18½'' x 12''

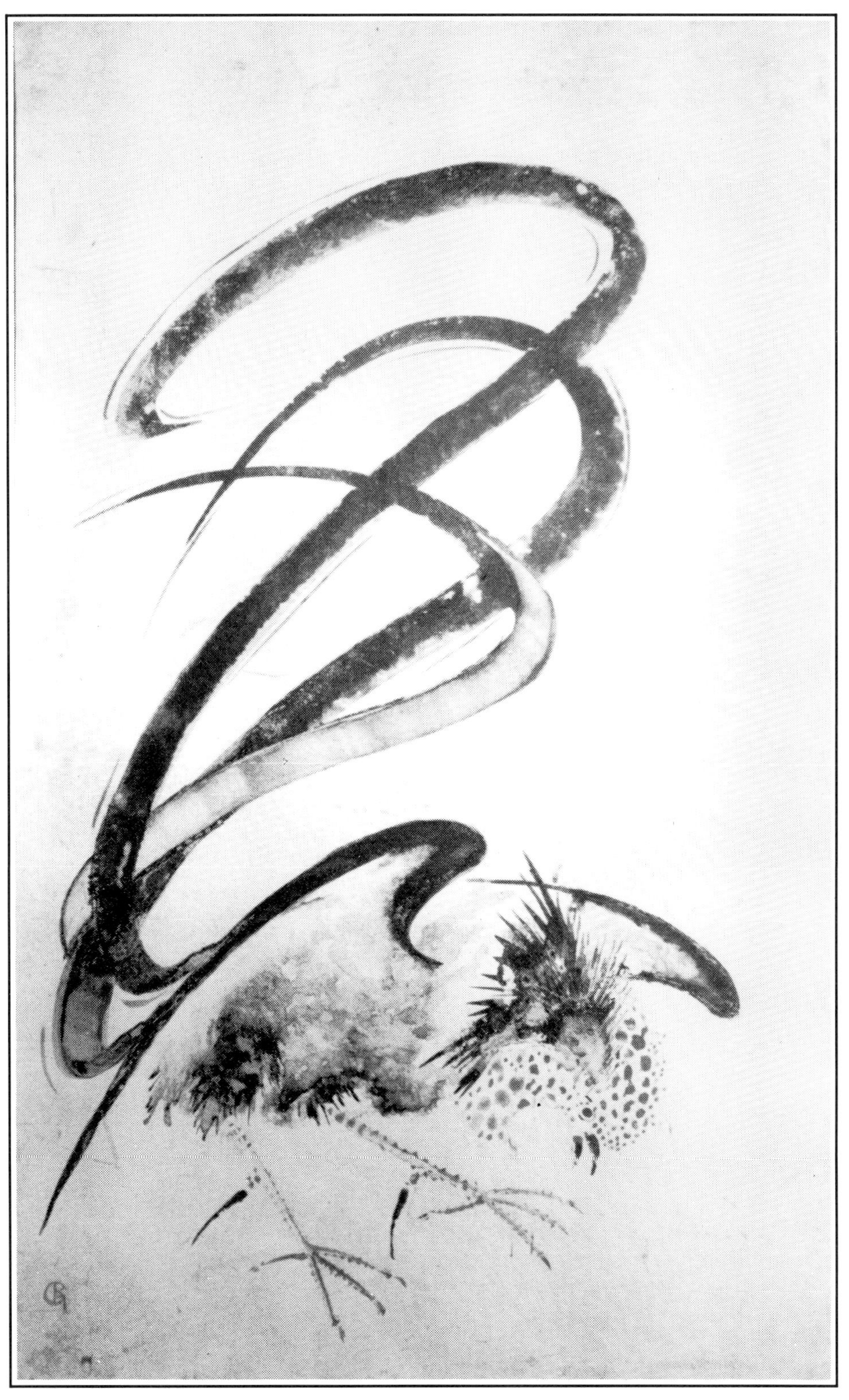

FIGHTING COCK ON GOLD LEAF (1948) 34'' x 23''

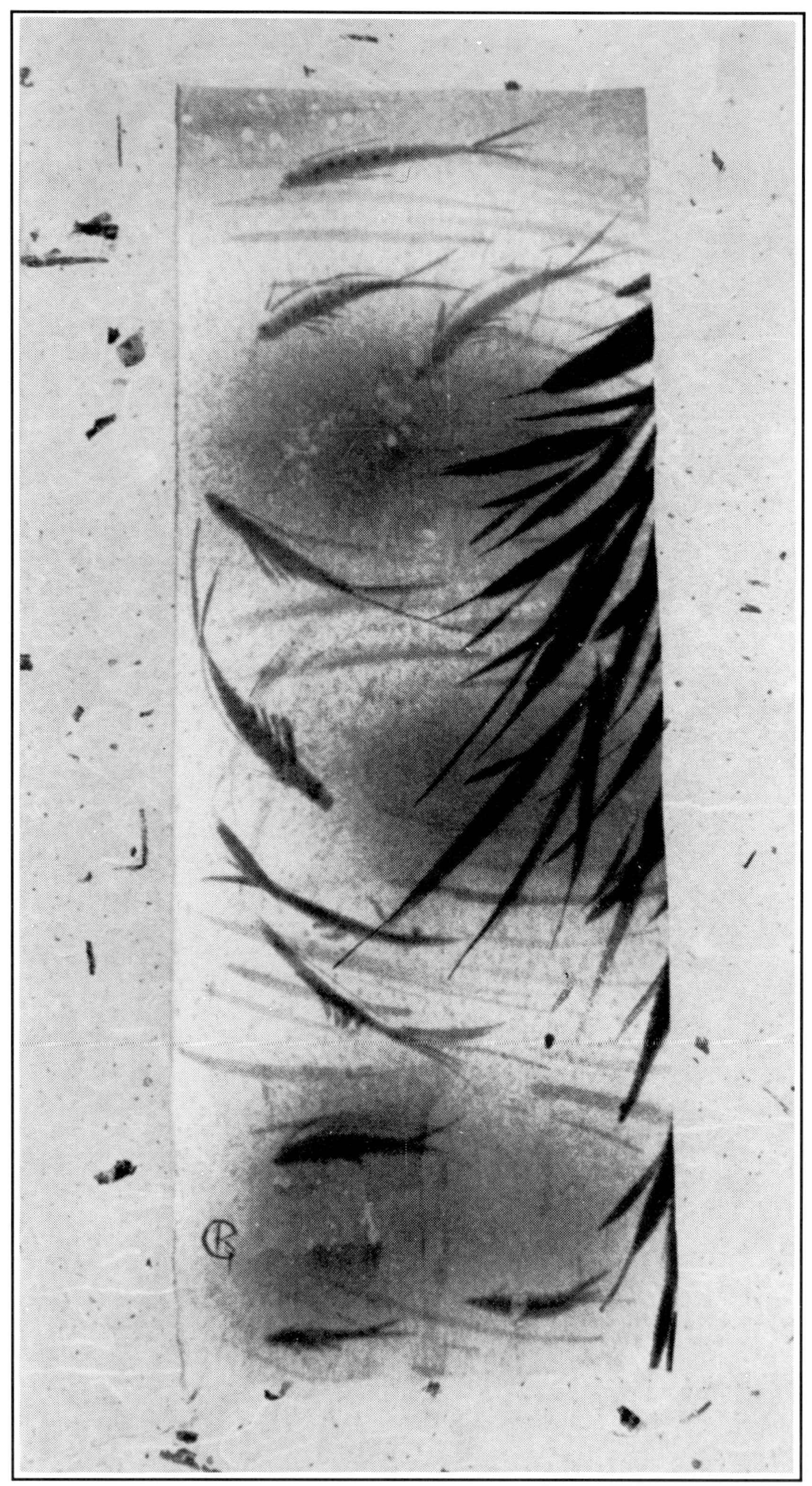

FISH (1958) 19½'' x 7½''

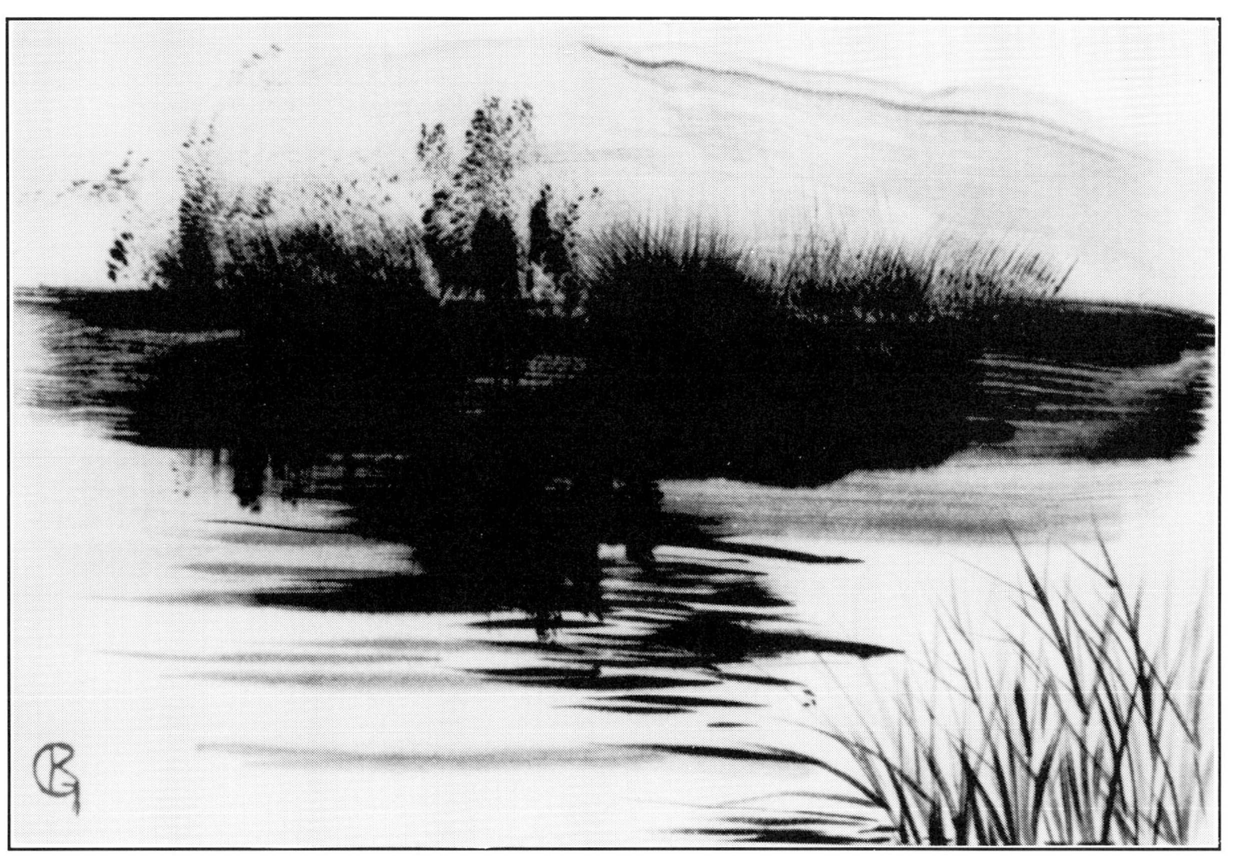

DAWN (1952) 11″ x 17″

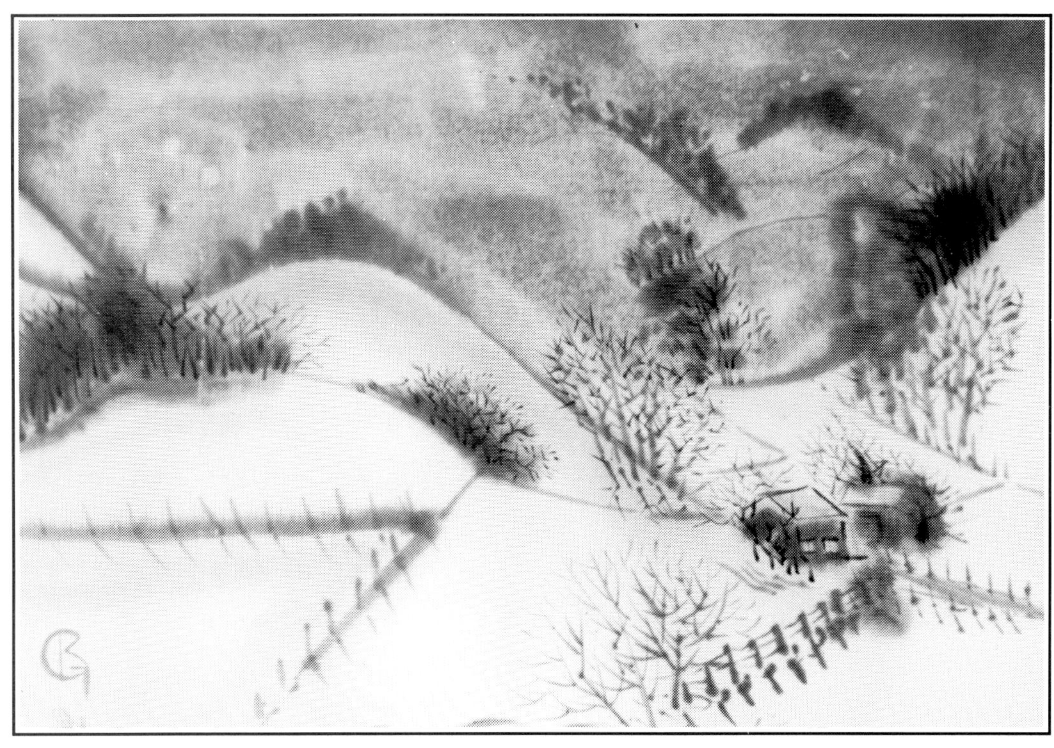

WINTER LANDSCAPE#1 (1952) 10'' x 15''

WINTER LANDSCAPE#2 (1952) 10'' x 15''

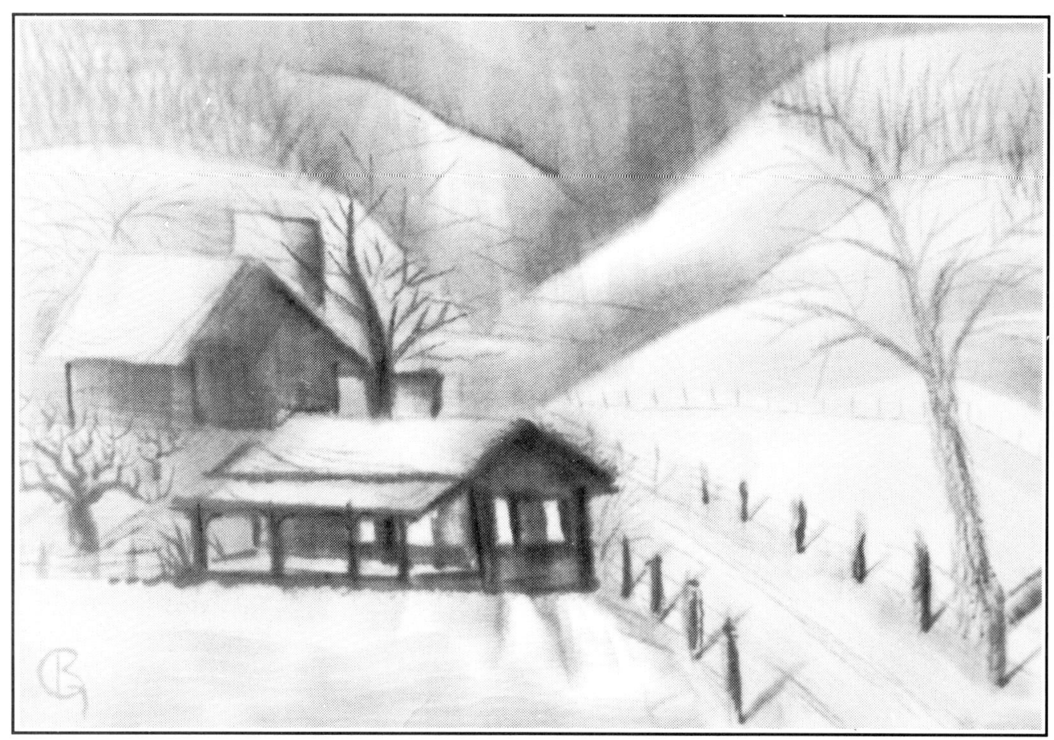

PRIVATE

In 1960 Boris and I bought an old ruin with thick crumbling walls, broken boarded-up windows, leaky roofs. Set among broken bottles, rusted tin cans, and barren ground, it was the answer to our dream of having an adobe in Santa Fe. Its restoration, and our discovery that it was an historic house, is a long story. It is enough to say here that, with hard work, over many years, it became a charming peaceful home for both of us and a perfect place for Boris to work. His touches are a very important part of the whole. This book would not be complete without them.

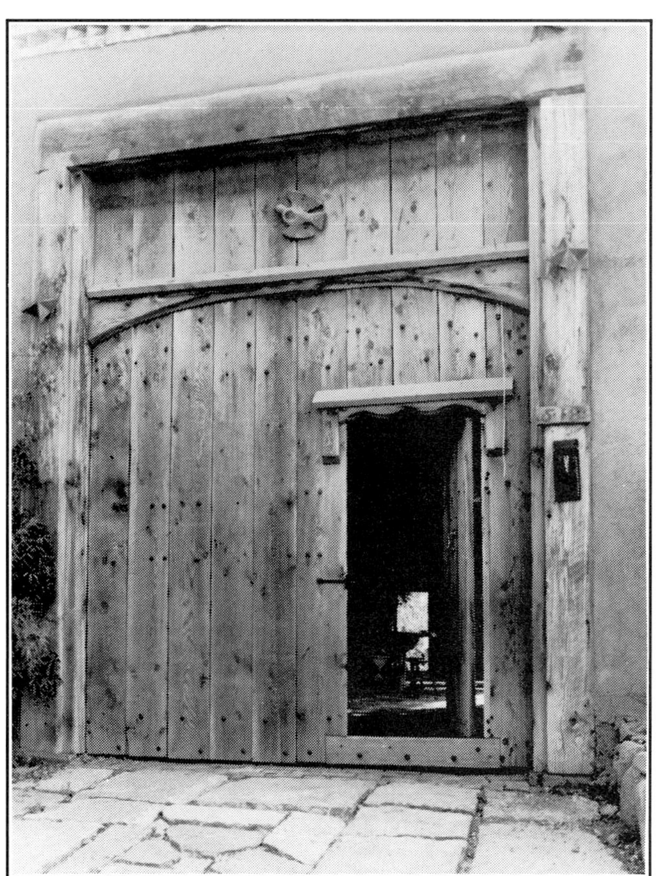

Front gate made by Gilbertson with 'Needle' door (1964), flagstone driveway laid by the artist

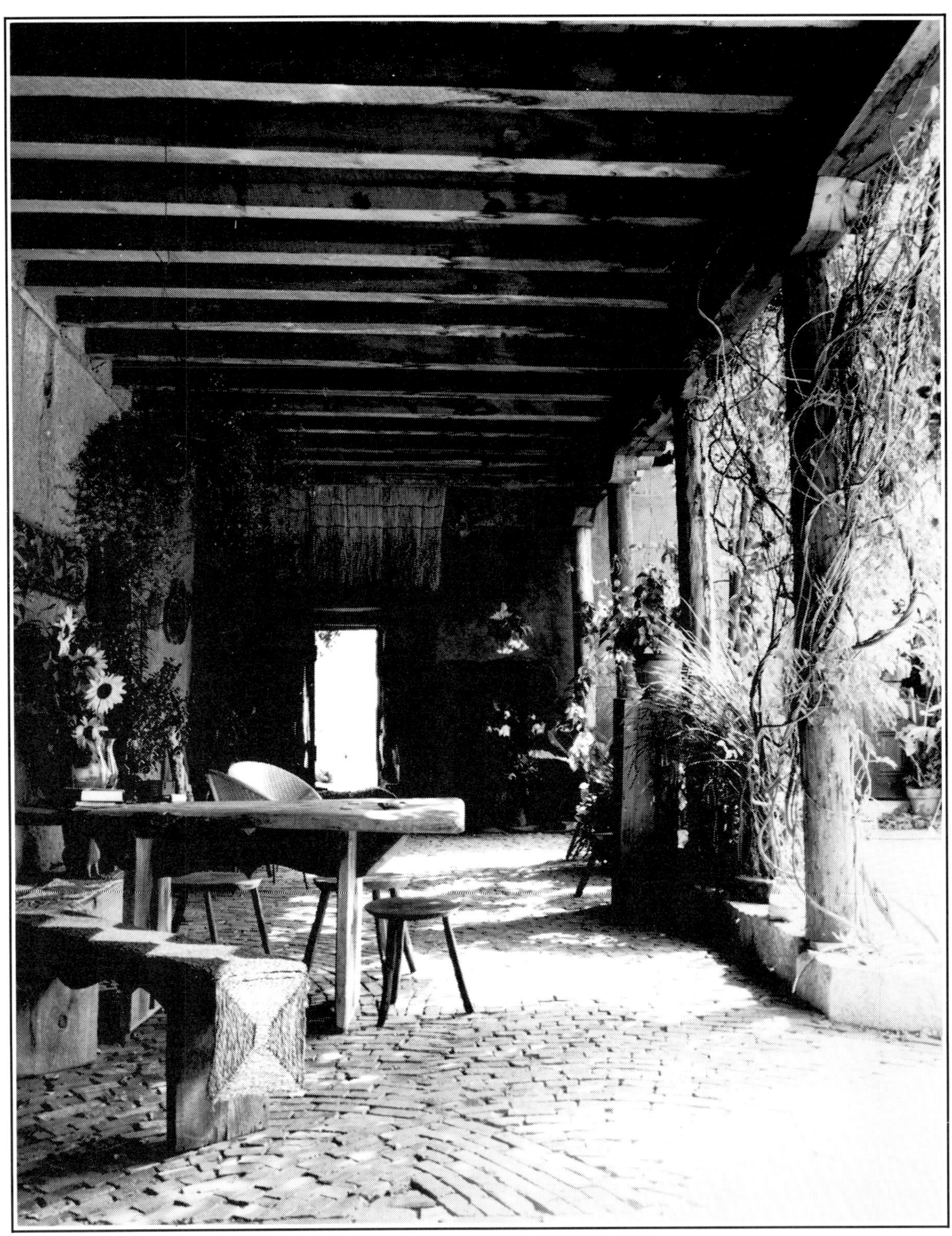

EL ZAGUAN, Running depth of house, east side of inner patio, rebuilt by the
artist in 1961; old high-fire bricks laid by Gilbertson in 1963, using the sides and ends

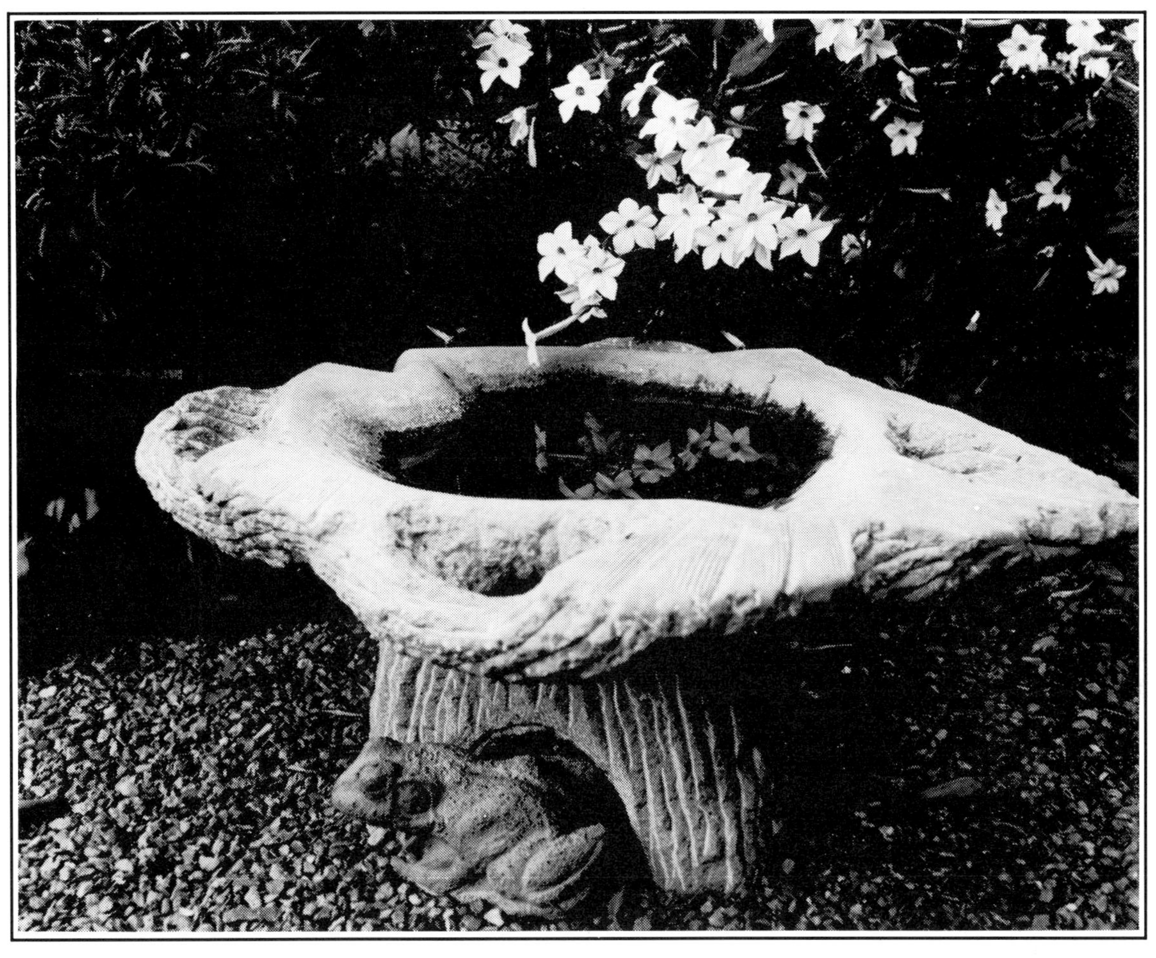

Birdbath in patio
carved limestone
(1952) 23″ x 11″

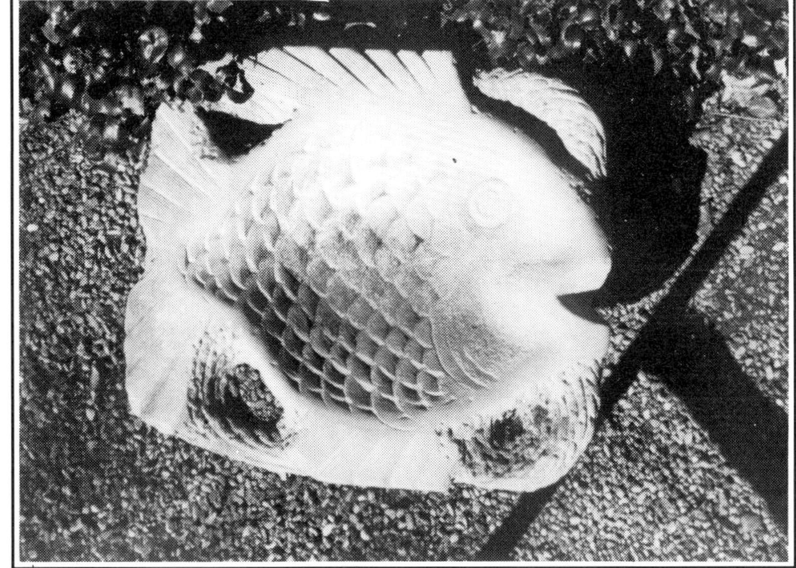

Detail of birdbath

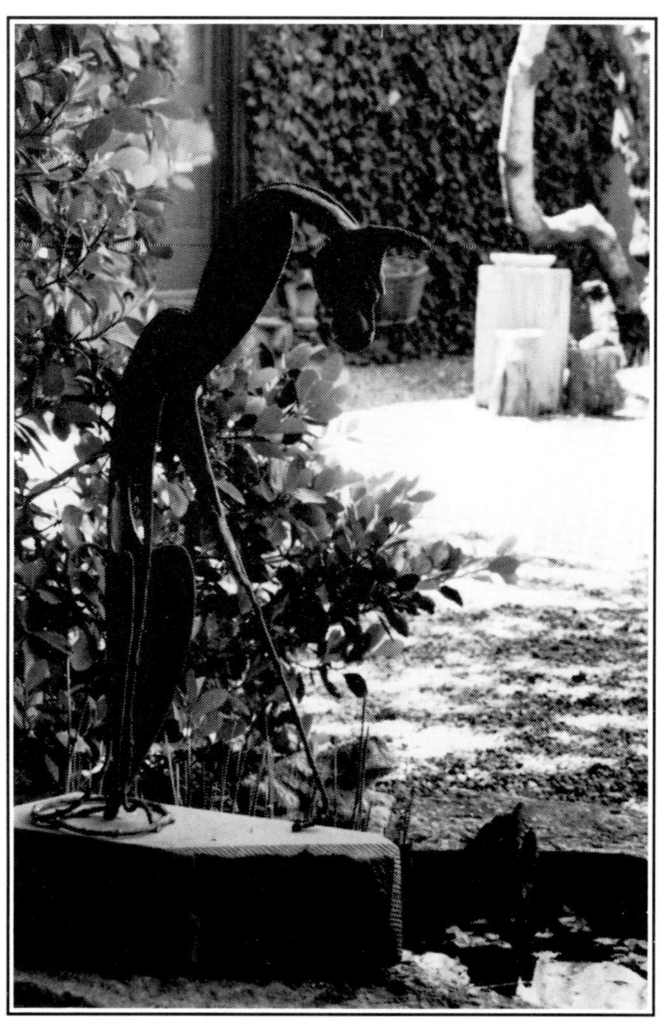

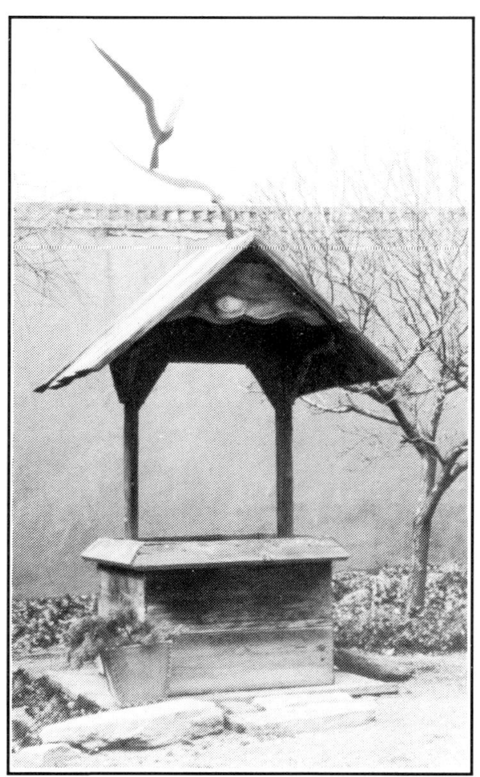

Cat in patio, copper (1955) 21''
FAIR OPHELIA'S HAND (in pool), copper (1965)

Wellhouse in patio (1962)
Birds, corten steel (1972) 6½'

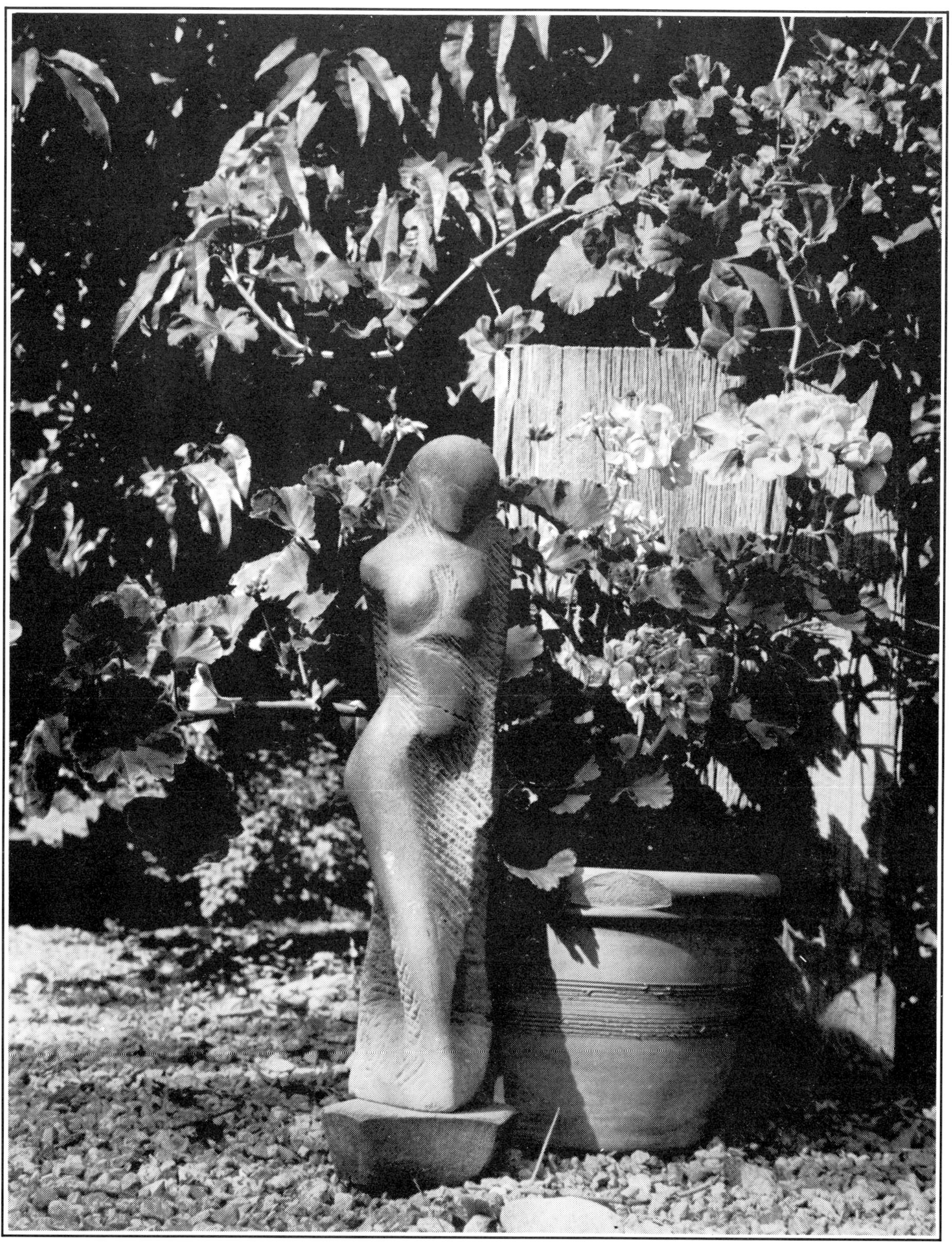

NUDE, carved limestone (1960) 18'' Photo: Mark Nohl

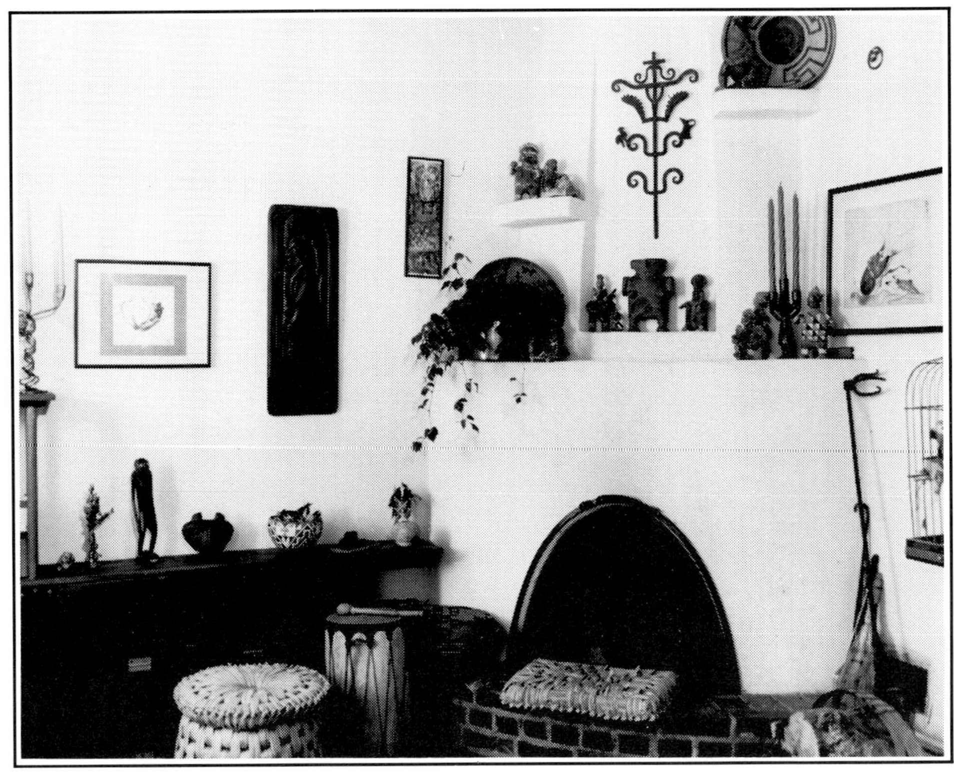

Fireplace in the *Sala* designed by the artist (1961)

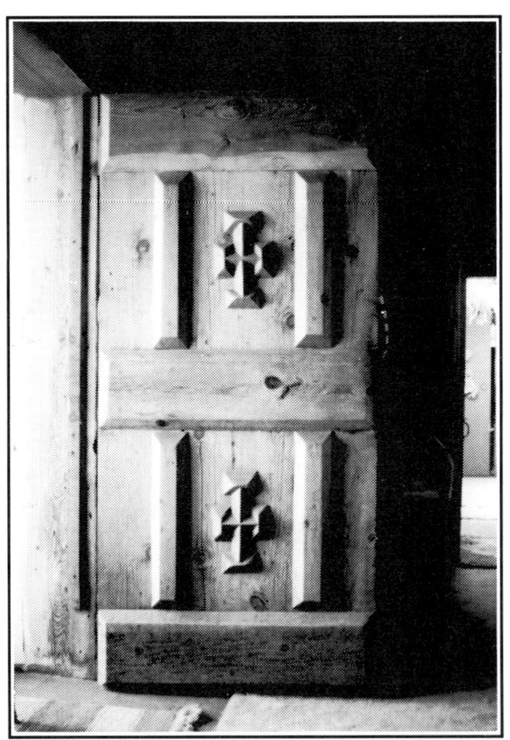

Door to rear portal (1961)

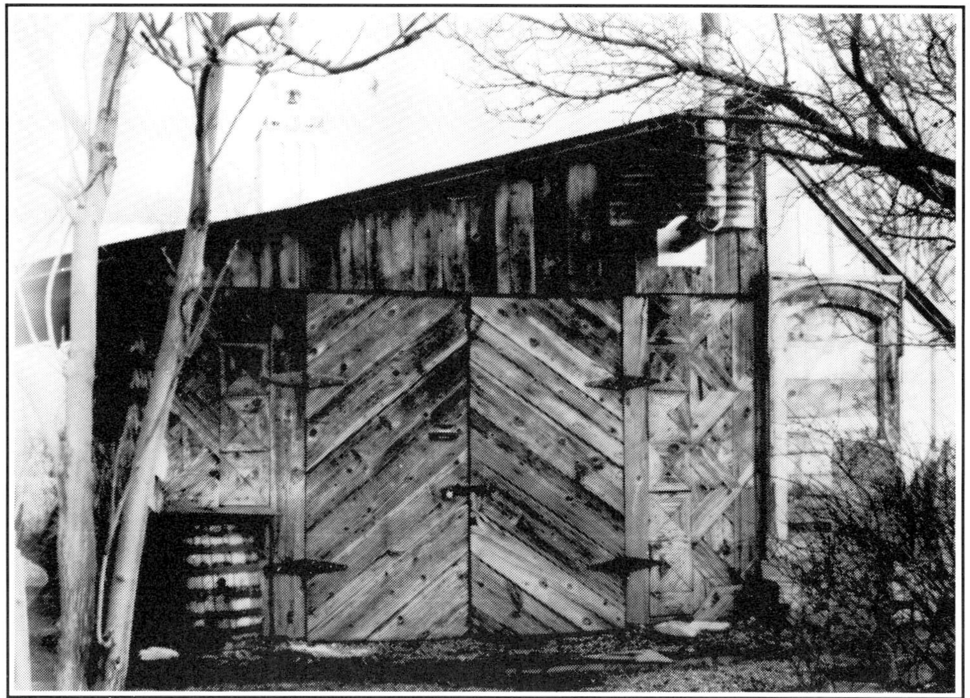

Gilbertson's workshop, weathered wood (1970)

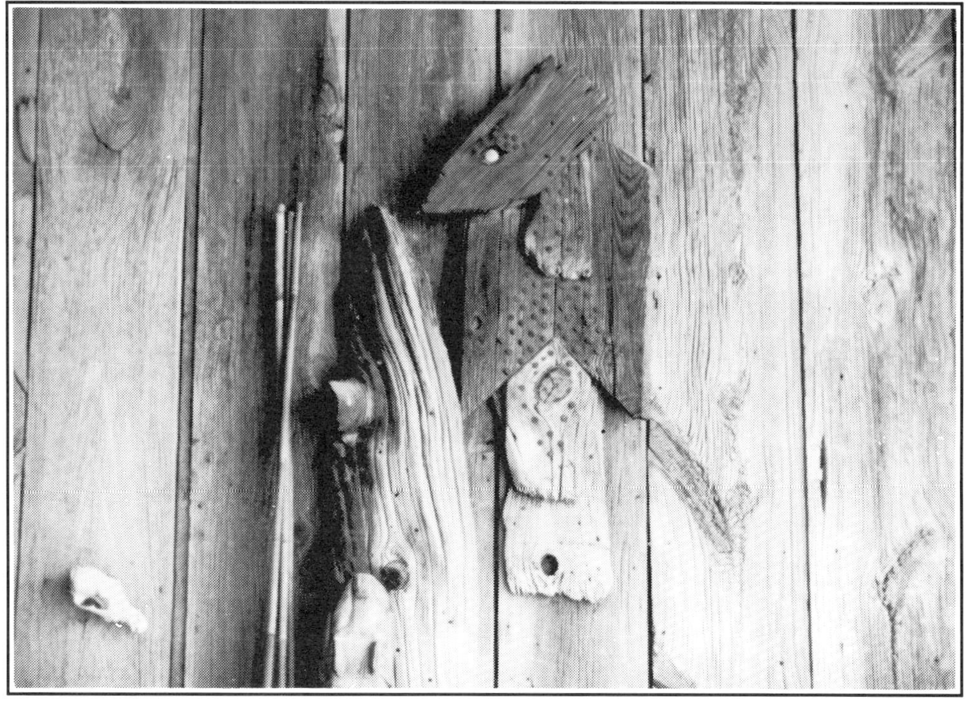

"AFFILIATED" WOODPECKER (1965) Outside wall of the artist's workshop,
weathered wood, large-headed brass nails, 38" x 18"

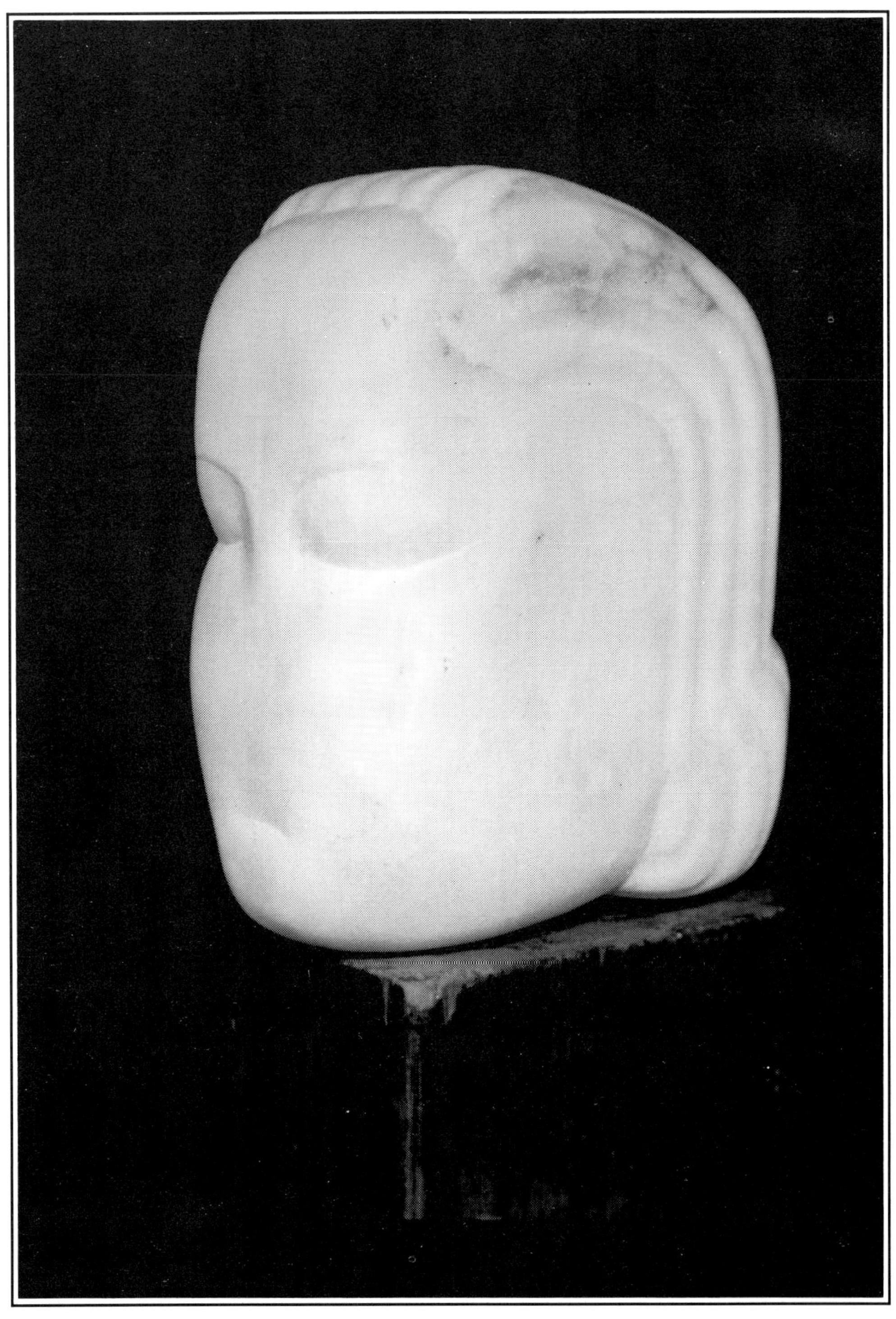

CHARLOTTE, marble (1930) 7'' x 5''

EXHIBITS

AWARDS

COMMISSIONS

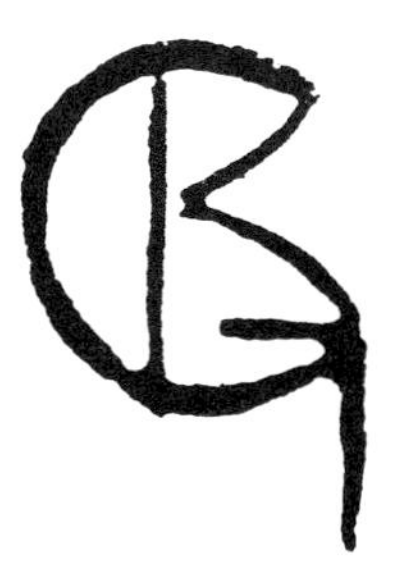

1933   PHILOSOPHER, Art Institute of Chicago. J.N. Eisendrath Prize. *(see page 8)*

1934   Invitation Show of Chicago Artists. Art Institute of Chicago.

1936   STONE BULL, Art Institute of Chicago. Alonzo C. Mather Prize. *(see page 13)*

1936   STONE RELIEF, Commission. Brookfield Zoo, Chicago.

1938   FISH LIMESTONE RELIEF, Commission. Post Office, Fond du Lac, Wisconsin. *(see page 15)*

1938   MARE AND COLT, Artists for Victory Exhibition. Metropolitan Museum, New York. *(see page 14)*

1939   MOOSE, BISON, Two Marble Reliefs. Commission. U.S. Department of the Interior, Washington, D.C. for Entrance Hall. *(see page 16)*

1946   MEMORIAL TO WOODS AND RIVER MEN, Commission. Wyoming Tie and Timber Co. *(see page 14)*

1947   STONE CARVING, Evanston, Illinois. Commission. Milwaukee, St. Paul, and Pacific Railway.

1951   FIGHTING BULLS, slate/gold leaf. American Sculpture Show. Metropolitan Museum, New York. *(see page 19)*

1957   STONE RELIEF AND TWO FREE-STANDING FIGURES, Commission. Maurice Webster, Architect for the Chess Pavilion, Lincoln Park, Chicago. *(see pages 23-26)*

1962   First Santa Fe, New Mexico, Show. Contemporaries Gallery.

1962   Barn Gallery, Santa Fe. Two-person Show.

1962   Gallery A, Taos, New Mexico. Two-person Show.

1962   Dallas Museum of Fine Arts, Dallas, Texas. Invitation Show.

1965   Marberg Gallery, El Paso, Texas. Exhibit Dedicated to Boris Gilbertson.

1966   Desert Southwest Art Gallery, Palm Desert, California. Three-person Show.

1967   Desert Southwest Art Gallery, Palm Desert, California. Two-person Show.

1967   Gallery A, Taos, New Mexico. Two-person Show.

1969   El Paso Museum of Art, El Paso, Texas. Two-person Show.

1969   SEABIRDS, Commission. American President Lines.

1969   PROPHET, Commission. Martha Schulselberg. El Paso, Texas. *(see page 31)*

1971   ELIJAH, Commission. Vivian Fiske, Santa Fe, New Mexico. Now at Fine Arts Museum, Santa Fe. *(see page 30)*

1973   BIRD MOBILE, Commission. Boeltcher Elementary School, Denver, Colorado.

1974   ODE TO BEATRIX POTTER, Donated to Le Bonheur Children's Medical Center. Memphis, Tennessee, 1982. *(see pages 42 – 43)*

1978   CHESS PIECES, Commission. Dr. John Fleming. *(see page 27)*